Data Handling

Interpreting Information

Ages 5–8

Peter Patilla & Paul Broadbent

Addison Wesley Longman Ltd
Edinburgh Gate
Harlow
Essex
CM20 2JE

England and Associated Companies throughout the World

© Addison Wesley Longman Limited 1997

The right of Peter Patilla and Paul Broadbent to be identified as the authors of this Work has been asserted by them in accordance with the Copyright, Designs and Patents Act of 1988.

This work is copyright, but copies may be made without fee or prior permission provided that the work has been paid for and such copies used solely within the institution for which the work is purchased. Works sent on approval or inspection and not yet paid for may not under any circumstances be copied. For copying in any other circumstances (e.g. by an external resource centre), prior written permission must be obtained from the Publishers and a fee may be payable.

ISBN 0582 31535 2

First published 1997

Designed by Ken Vail Graphic Design

Printed in Singapore

The Publisher's policy is to use paper manufactured from sustainable forests.

Contents

Topic	Activity sheets
Tally Charts	1–4
Display	5–8
Venn Diagrams	9–12
Carroll Diagrams	13–16
Mappings	17–20
Decision Trees	21–24
Charts/Lists & Tables	25–28
Databases	29–32
Pictograms	33–36
Bar Graph 1:1	37–40
Bar Graph 1:2	41–44
Bar Graph 1:10	45–48
Comparison Graphs	49–52
Answers	
Record Sheet	

Data Handling

Opportunities for handling data can arise from mathematical or cross-curricular activities which are relevant to the pupils.

The data-handling process can be shown in five simple steps:

1. Posing questions
2. Collecting and recording information
3. Organising information
4. Displaying information
5. Interpreting and deducing information

In order to develop a proficiency in handling data pupils often need to develop one skill in isolation from others.

The activities in this book focus upon the skill of interpreting and deducing information from a variety of displays. It is recognised that this type of work on its own will not develop the complete data-handling process.

Farm Animals

1 Draw ticks to match the animals. ✓

2 How many horses? ....

3 How many lambs? ....

4 How many sheep? ....

5 How many cows and calves altogether? ....

6 Which animal was there most of? ....

Data Handling Book 1 © Addison Wesley Longman Limited 1997

| Name | Class |

Lunch Boxes

2 Tally Charts

Here is what ten children had in their lunch boxes.

sandwiches						
rolls							
crisps				
fruit						
biscuits		
drinks									

1. How many rolls were there? ....
2. How many drinks were there? ....
3. How many crisps and biscuits were there? ....
4. Were there more sandwiches than rolls? ....
5. Did everyone have a drink? ....
6. Did anyone have more than one roll or one sandwich? ....

Data Handling Book 1 © Addison Wesley Longman Limited 1997

Name   Class

Collecting Litter

3 TALLY CHARTS

The table shows litter collected.

		Total
paper and card	卌 卌 卌 |||	
metal	卌 卌 ||	
glass	卌 |||	
plastic	卌 卌 卌		
other things	卌 ||||	

1. Write the totals in the table.

2. How many plastic objects were collected? ....

3. How many metal objects were collected? ....

4. What do you think *other things* could be? ....

....

CHALLENGE How many pieces of litter were collected altogether?

Data Handling Book 1   © Addison Wesley Longman Limited 1997

Name　　　　　　　　　　　　Class

Birthday Days

4　Tally Charts

This table shows how many birthdays fell on each day of the week.

Day	Tally	Total
Monday	||||　||||　||	
Tuesday	||||　||||　||||　||||	
Wednesday	||||　||||　||||	
Thursday	||||　||||	
Friday	||||　||||　||||　||||　||||	
Saturday	||||　||||　|||	
Sunday	||||　||||　||	

1 Write the totals in the table.

2 How many birthdays fell on a Wednesday?　..........................

3 How many birthdays fell on a Tuesday?　..........................

4 Which day has the most birthdays?　..........................

5 Which two days have the same number of birthdays?　..........................

6 Was a class or a school asked about birthdays?　..........................

Data Handling Book 1　　　　© Addison Wesley Longman Limited 1997

| Name | Class |

Fruit Bar

5 DISPLAY

1. What is the cost of a pear? ....
2. Which piece of fruit costs 15p? ....
3. What is the cost of two oranges? ....
4. Which two fruits would cost 8p? ....
5. What is the cost of an apple and a pear? ....
6. Which things you could buy with 15p? ....

   or ....

   or ....

Data Handling Book 1 © Addison Wesley Longman Limited 1997

Clothes Shop

1. What would a striped T-shirt cost? ....

2. Which is the dearer baseball cap? ....

3. Which sunglasses cost £7? ....

4. How much more are the spotted socks then the plain socks? ....

5. What would a FAN T-shirt and plain socks cost altogether? ....

6. Which items could you buy for exactly £10? ....

　　or ....

　　or ....

Data Handling Book 1

| Name | Class |

Book Shop

DISPLAY 7

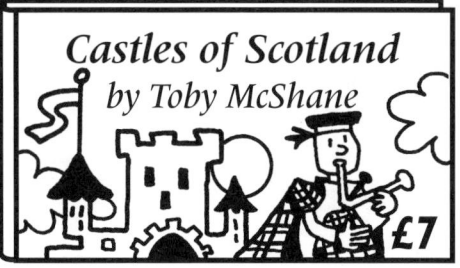

1 Who wrote about the lost horse? ....

2 Which book did Will Marriott write? ....

3 Which book cost the most? ....

4 Which book did Lucy Hall write? ....

5 How much would the books on *Castles* and *Nursery Rhymes* cost together? ....

6 Which two books are storybooks? ....

Data Handling Book 1 © Addison Wesley Longman Limited 1997

| Name | Class |

Multiscreen Cinemas

8 DISPLAY

Screen 1
Screen 2
Screen 3
Screen 4

| all week | Wed, Thur, Fri | Mon to Fri | Sat & Sun |

£2
Start 6.30 pm
8.30 pm

£3
Start 8.00 pm

£2.50
Start 6.00 pm
7.30 pm

£4
Start 3.00 pm
5.00 pm
8.00 pm

 1 Which film is the most expensive to see? ....

 2 Which films can I see on Saturday? ....

 3 Which films start after 7.30 pm? ....

 4 Which film can I see before 6 o'clock? ....

 5 Which screen will be open most during a week? ....

6 How many times will the film on Screen 3 be shown during one week? ....

Data Handling Book 1 © Addison Wesley Longman Limited 1997

Name .... Class ....

Fruit Sorts

9 VENN DIAGRAMS

(eat the skin)

grapes

orange

apples

pears

banana

pineapple

1 Look at the diagram and name two fruits which have skin you can eat.

.... and ....

2 Look at the diagram and name two fruits which have skin you cannot eat.

.... and ....

3 Write these fruits on the diagram: cherries
melons

Can you write the names of two more fruits on the diagram?

Data Handling Book 1   © Addison Wesley Longman Limited 1997

Name   Class

Number Sort

10 VENN DIAGRAMS

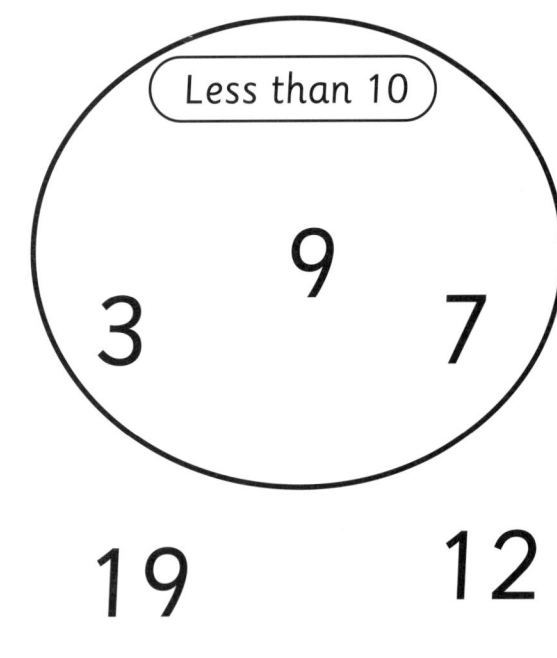
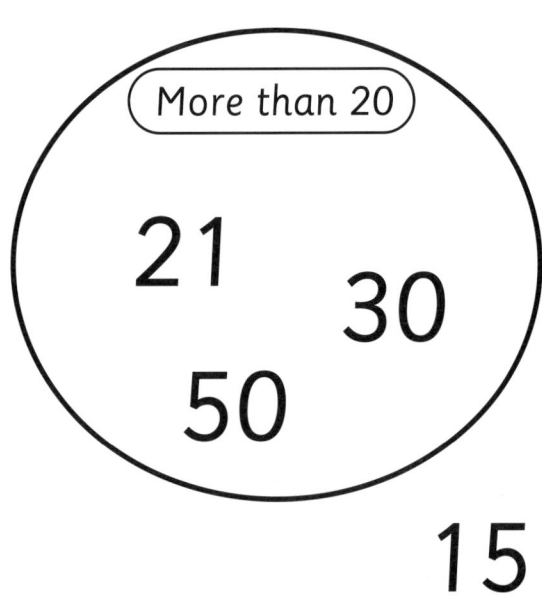

Less than 10: 3, 9, 7

More than 20: 21, 30, 50

19   12   15

1 Look at the diagram and write two numbers which are more than twenty.

.... and ....

2 Look at the diagram and write two numbers which are less than ten.

.... and ....

3 Write two numbers on the diagram which are not less than ten but not more than twenty.

CHALLENGE Write these numbers on the diagram.   62, 5, 16

Data Handling Book 1   © Addison Wesley Longman Limited 1997

| Name | Class |

People Sort

11 VENN DIAGRAMS

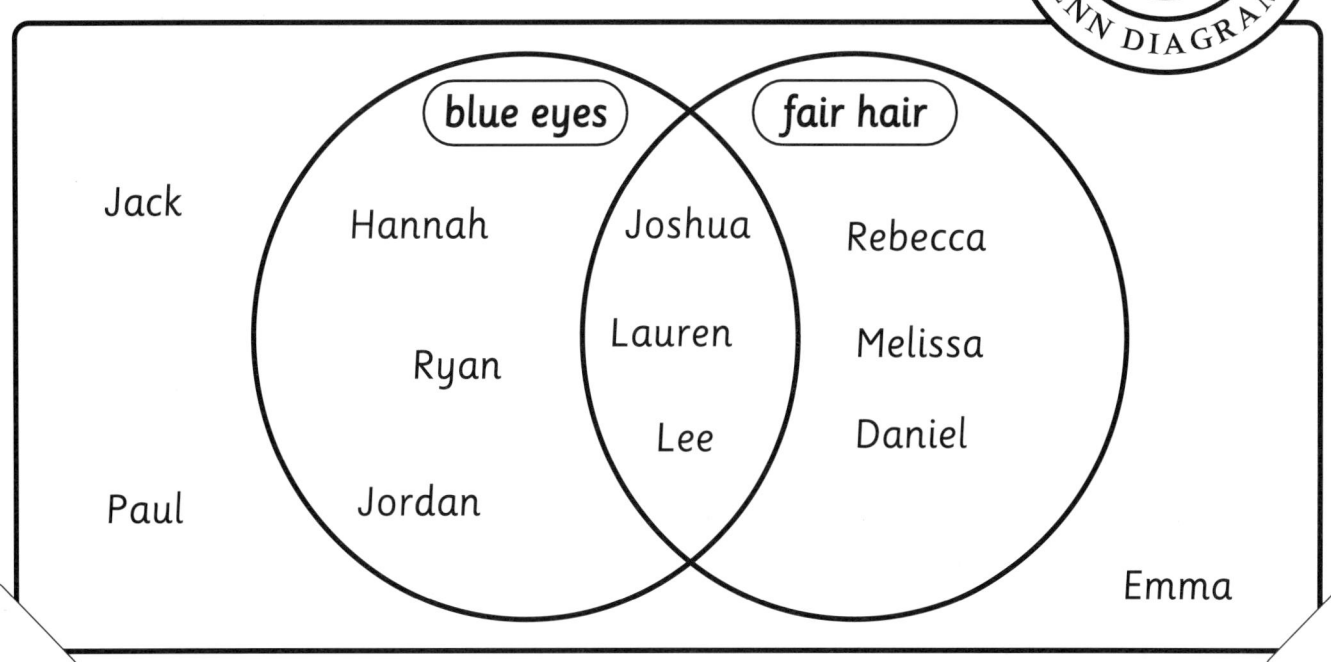

From the diagram name someone who has:

1 blue eyes and fair hair ....

2 fair hair and not blue eyes ....

3 blue eyes but not fair hair ....

4 not fair hair nor blue eyes ....

What do you know about:

5 Jordan? ....

6 Jack? ....

7 Melissa? ....

8 Lauren? ....

 Simon has brown eyes and ginger hair. Write his name on the diagram.

Data Handling Book 1 © Addison Wesley Longman Limited 1997

Name	Class	

Shape Sorts

12 VENN DIAGRAMS

KEY
- ▭ rectangle
- □ square
- ◇ diamond
- △ arrow head
- △ triangle
- ○ circle
- ⬠ pentagon

(Venn diagram: outer circle "Four sides" contains rectangle and diamond; inner circle "Squares" contains a square. Outside the circles: circle, triangle, arrow head, pentagon.)

1 From the diagram, name two shapes which have four sides but are not squares.

.... and ....

2 From the diagram, name two shapes which do not have four sides.

.... and ....

3 Draw these shapes on the diagram. ▱ ⬭

CHALLENGE Draw two four-sided shapes of your own on the diagram.

Data Handling Book 1 © Addison Wesley Longman Limited 1997

Name   Class

Vegetable Sort

13 CARROLL DIAGRAMS

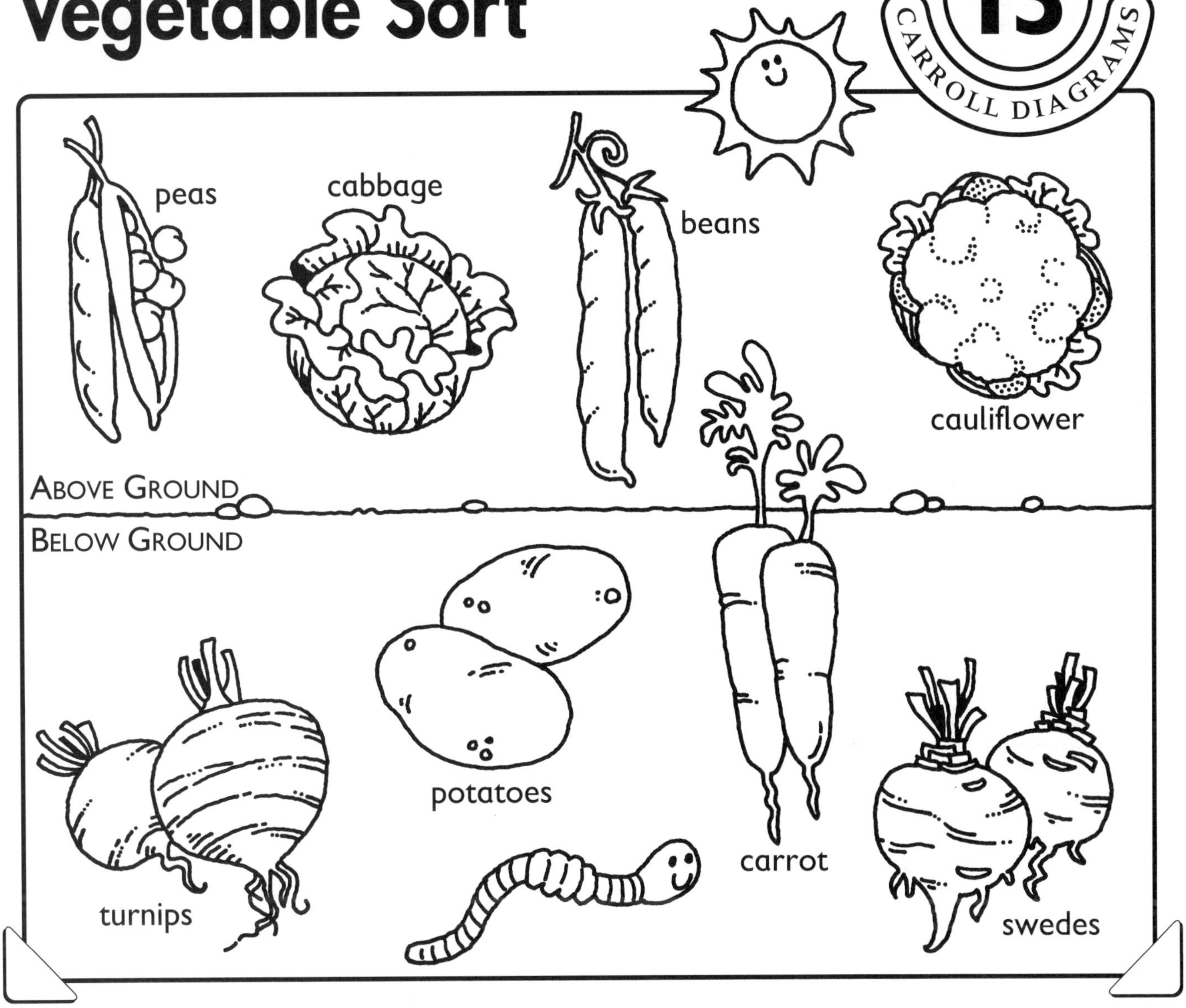

ABOVE GROUND: peas, cabbage, beans, cauliflower

BELOW GROUND: turnips, potatoes, carrot, swedes

1) Where do turnips grow? ....

2) Where do cabbages grow? ....

3) Which vegetables do not grow above ground? ....

4) Name a vegetable which grows above ground. ....

 CHALLENGE Write the names of two more vegetables on the diagram.

Data Handling Book 1   © Addison Wesley Longman Limited 1997

Shape Boxes

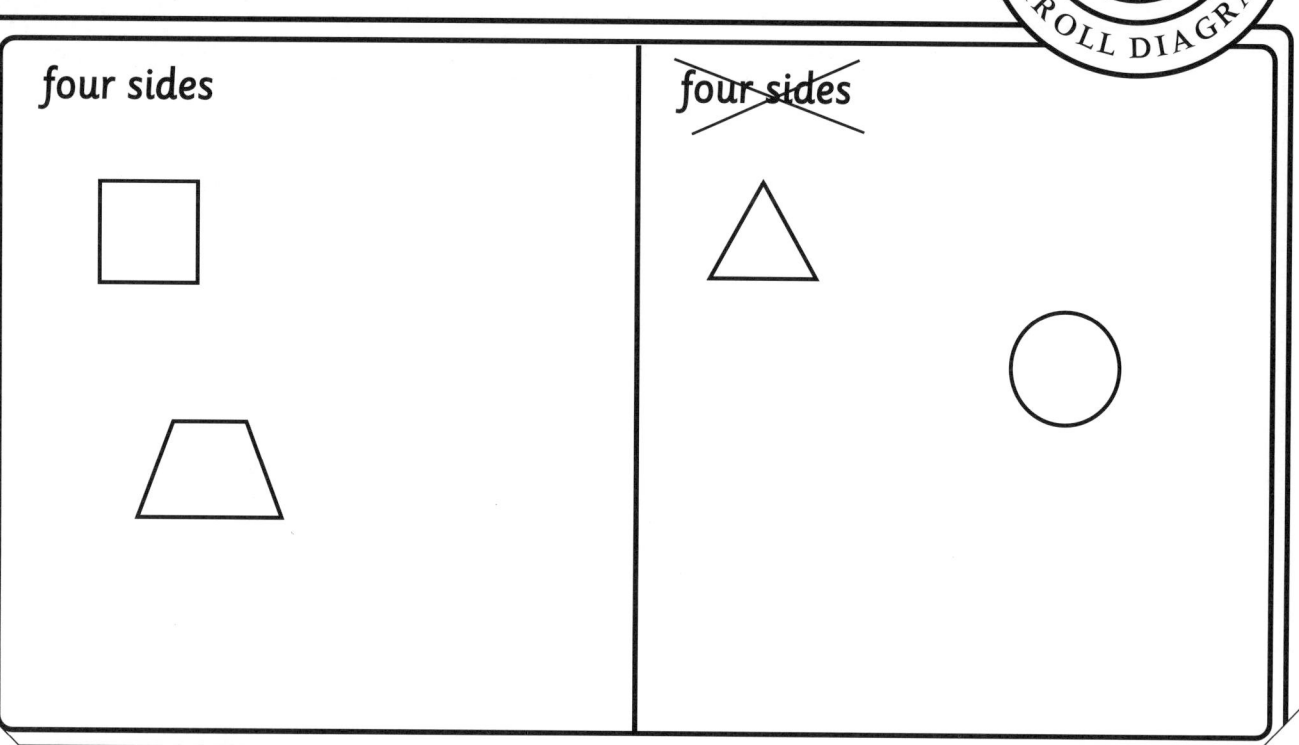

Draw these shapes on the diagram.

 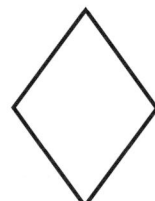   

    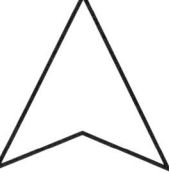

 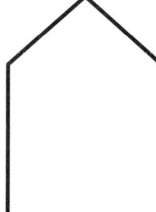   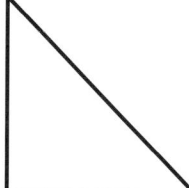

 Draw a shape of your own which will go into the ~~four sides~~ box.

Name   Class

Shoe Sort

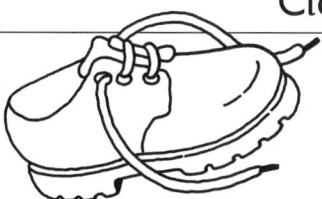

15 CARROLL DIAGRAMS

	laces	not laces	
	William, Sophie	Amy, Elena, Ian	brown
	Matthew, Ravi, Vicky	Lisa, James	not brown

From the diagram name someone who is wearing:

1 laces but not brown shoes ....

2 brown shoes which do not have laces ....

3 brown lace-up shoes ....

What do you know about the shoes of:

4 Elena? ....

5 Lisa? ....

6 Matthew? ....

CHALLENGE

George is wearing green trainers with laces.
Write his name on the diagram.

Data Handling Book 1   © Addison Wesley Longman Limited 1997

Name   Class

Card Sorting

Some cards have been sorted.

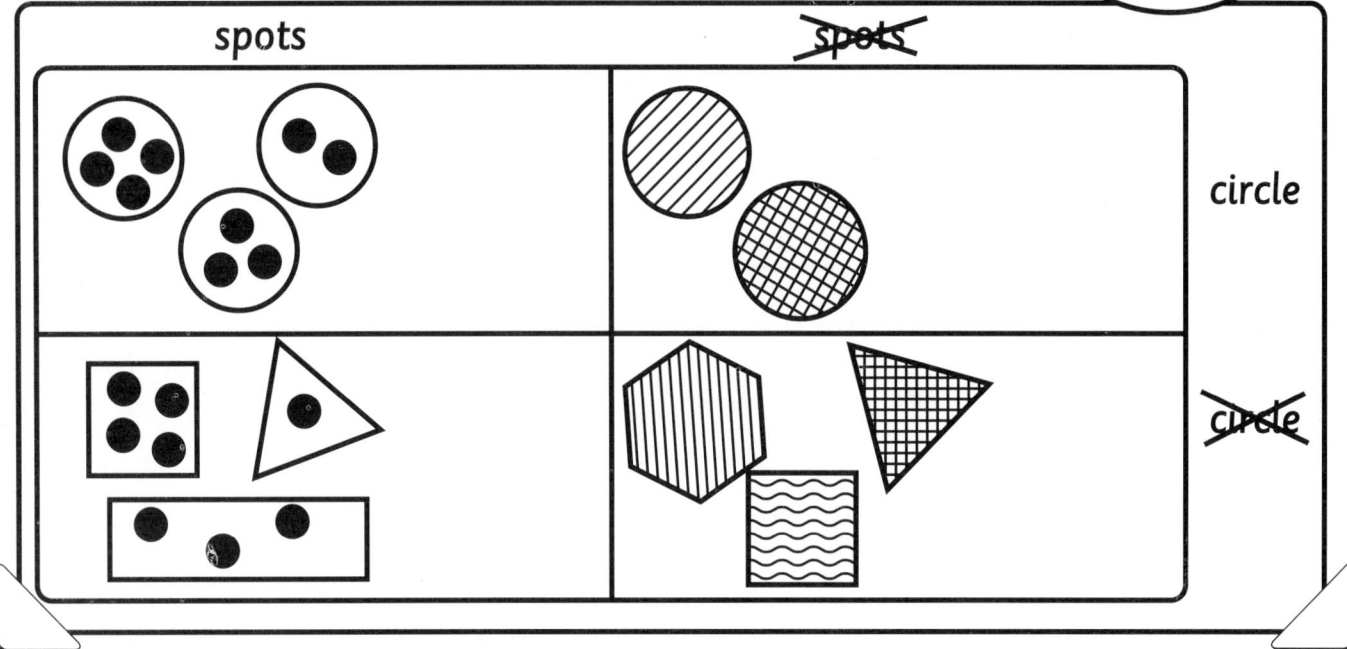

1. How many circle cards are there? ....
2. How many cards with spots? ....
3. How many cards do not have spots? ....
4. How many circle cards with spots are there? ....
5. How many cards are not circles and have no spots? ....
6. How many cards altogether? ....

 Draw these cards on the diagram.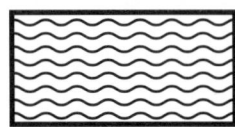

Data Handling Book 1   © Addison Wesley Longman Limited 1997

Sports

Here are the sports played by some teachers.

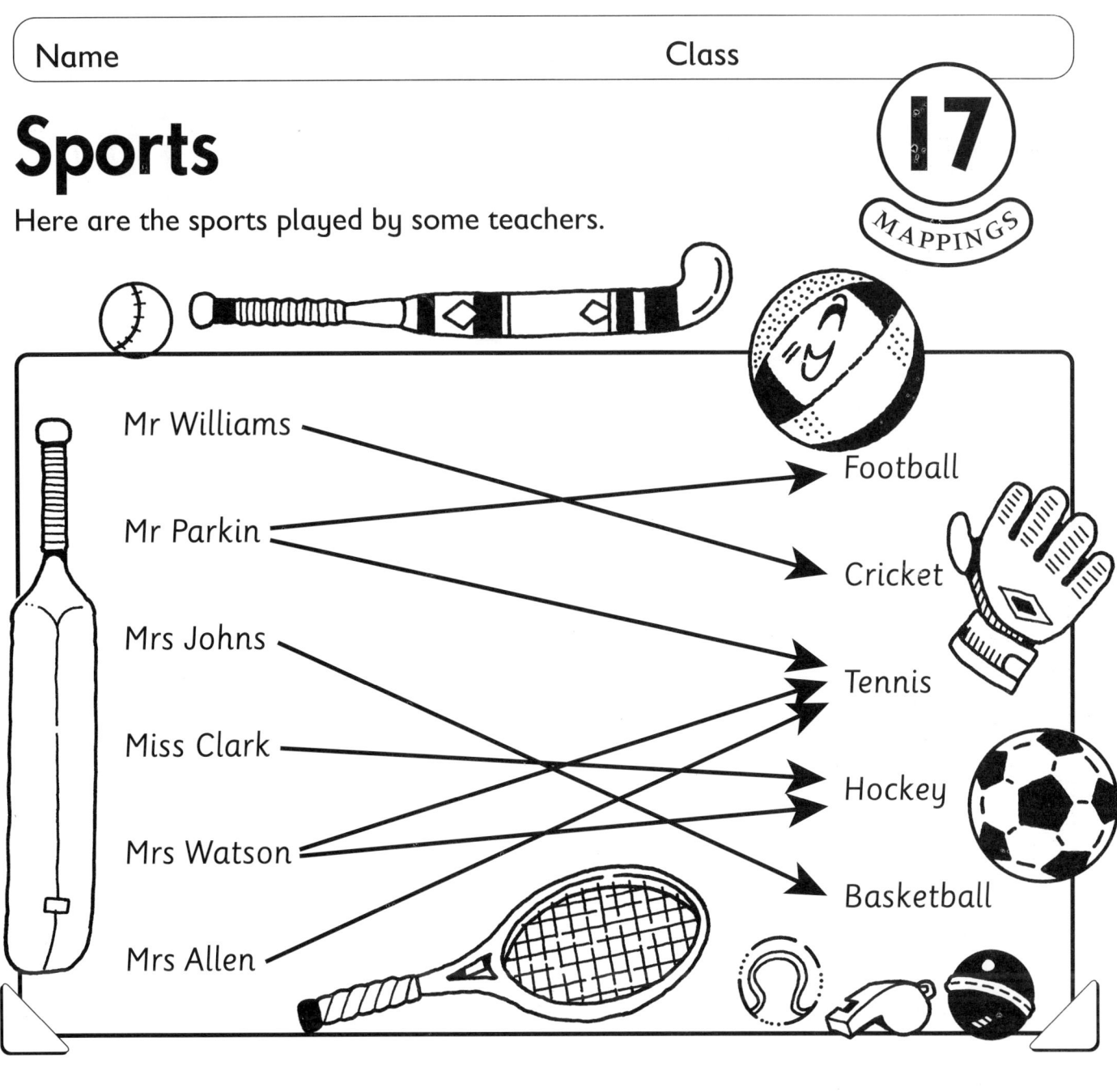

1. Which sport does Mrs Allen play? ....
2. Which sports does Mr Parkin play? ....
3. Who plays hockey? ....
4. Who plays cricket? ....
5. Which sport is played by most people? ....
6. Which two sports does Mrs Watson play? ....

| Name | Class |

Where We Live

18 MAPPINGS

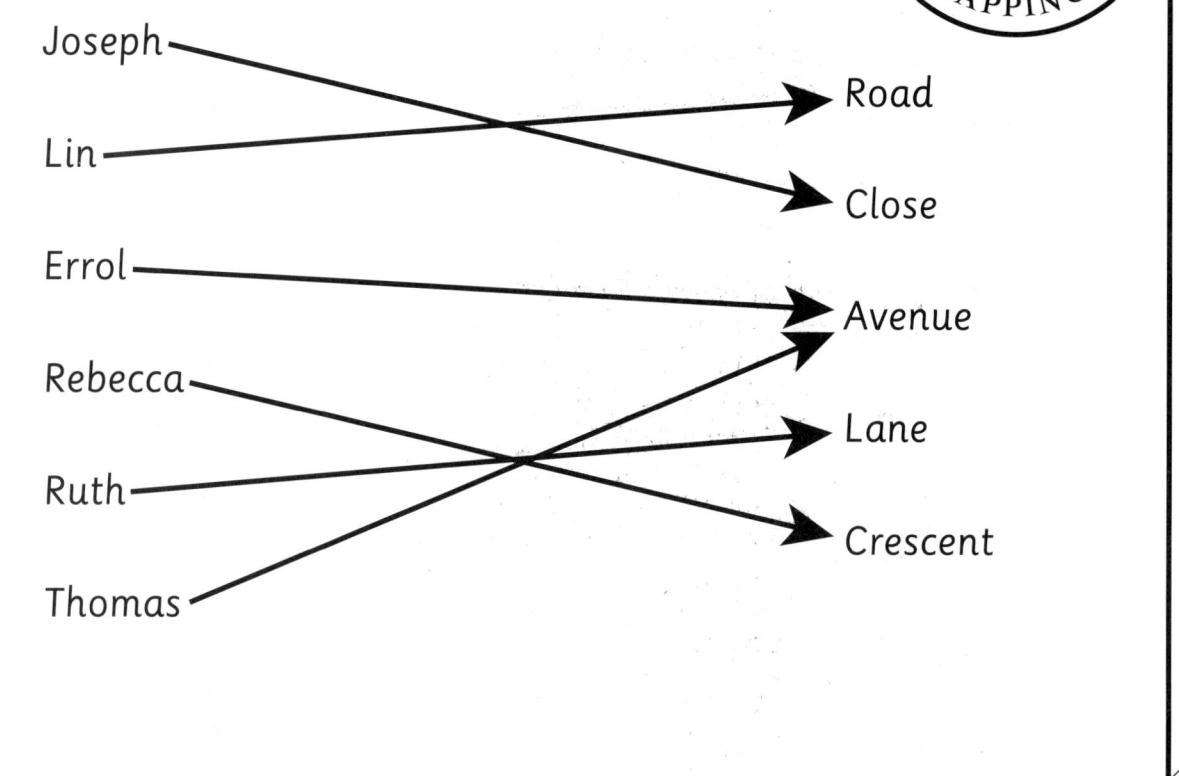

From the diagram:

1 Who lives on a close? ....

2 Who lives on a crescent? ....

3 Where does Errol live? ....

4 Where does Thomas live? ....

5 How many people live on an avenue? ....

6 How many people were asked where they lived? ....

? CHALLENGE Mira lives at Simmons Lane. Write her name with an arrow on the diagram.

Data Handling Book 1 © Addison Wesley Longman Limited 1997

Name　　　　　　　　　　　Class

Instruments

19 MAPPINGS

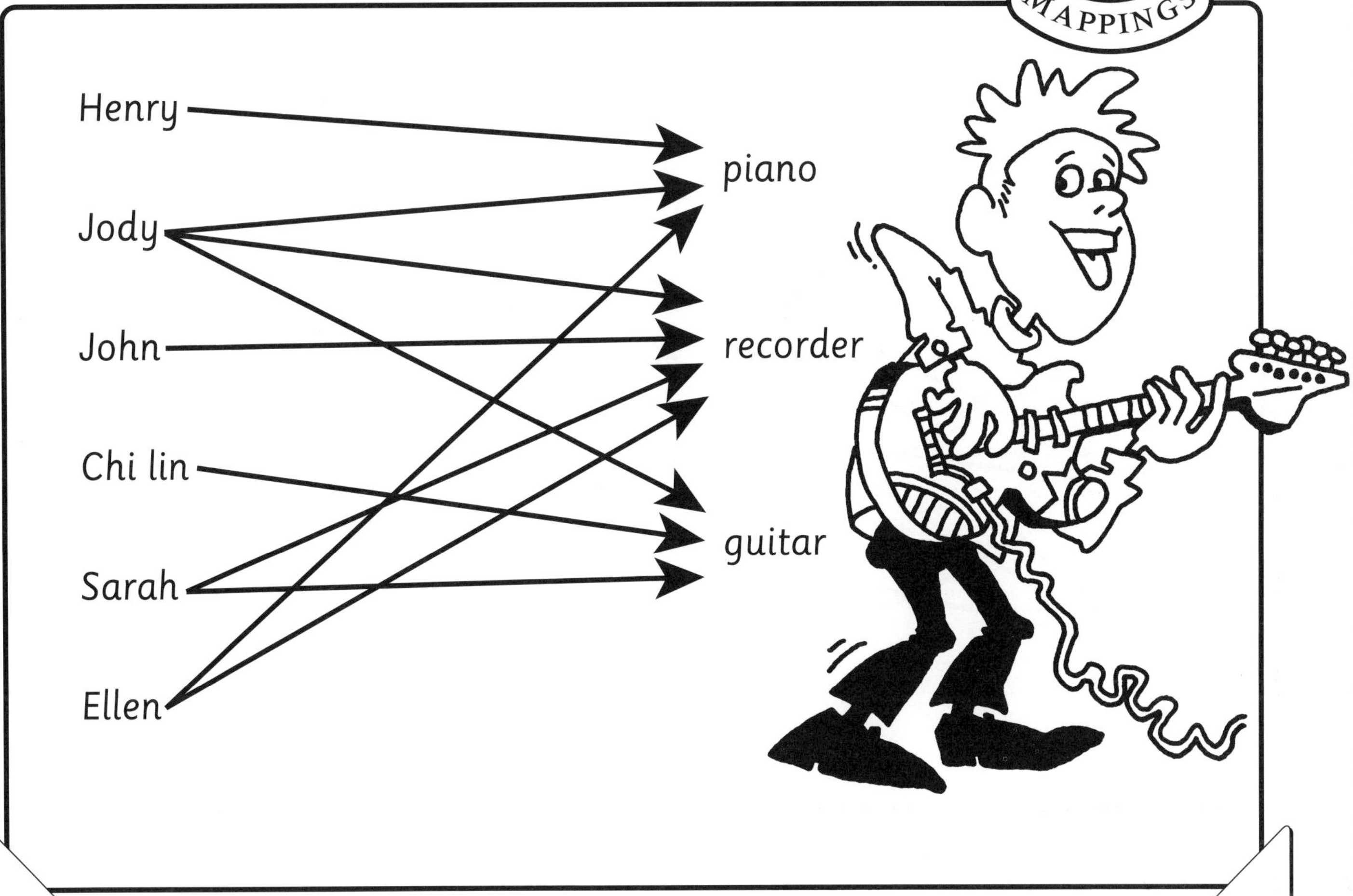

Henry — piano
Jody
John — recorder
Chi lin
Sarah — guitar
Ellen

1. What does Henry play? ....
2. What does Ellen play? ....
3. Who plays the piano? ....
4. Who plays the recorder? ....
5. How many people play the guitar? ....
6. Which instrument was played by most children? ....

CHALLENGE Kim plays the recorder and piano.
Write her name with arrows on the diagram.

Data Handling Book 1　　　　　　　　© Addison Wesley Longman Limited 1997

Name　　　　　　　　　Class

Our Lunch

20 MAPPINGS

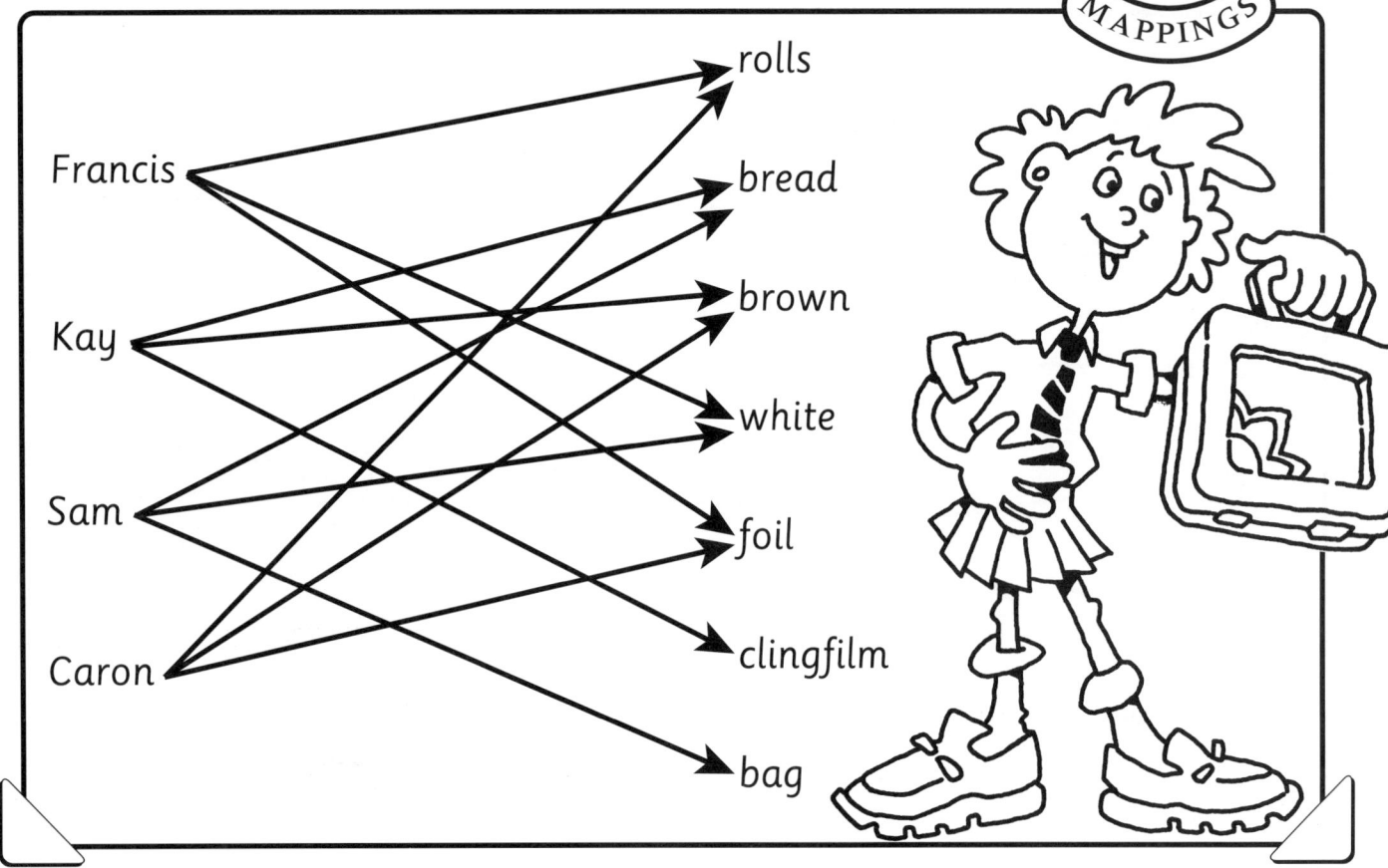

1. Who had their lunch wrapped in a bag?　..................................
2. Who had bread for their lunch?　..................................
3. Who had white rolls for lunch?　..................................
4. How was Sam's lunch wrapped?　..................................
5. Did Caron have brown or white rolls?　..................................
6. How many people had their lunch wrapped in a bag?　..................................
7. Who had brown bread wrapped in clingfilm?　..................................
8. Who had their lunch wrapped in foil?　..................................

Data Handling Book 1　　　　　© Addison Wesley Longman Limited 1997

Name _____ Class _____

Fruit Tree

21 DECISION TREES

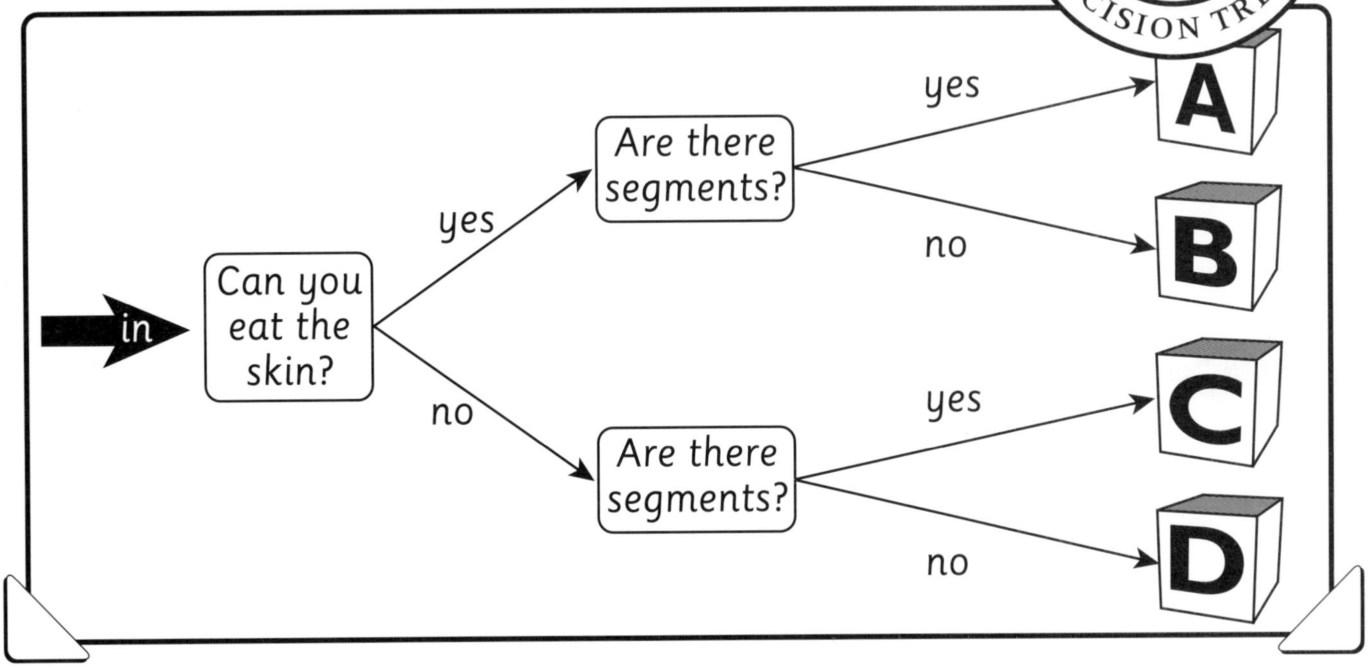

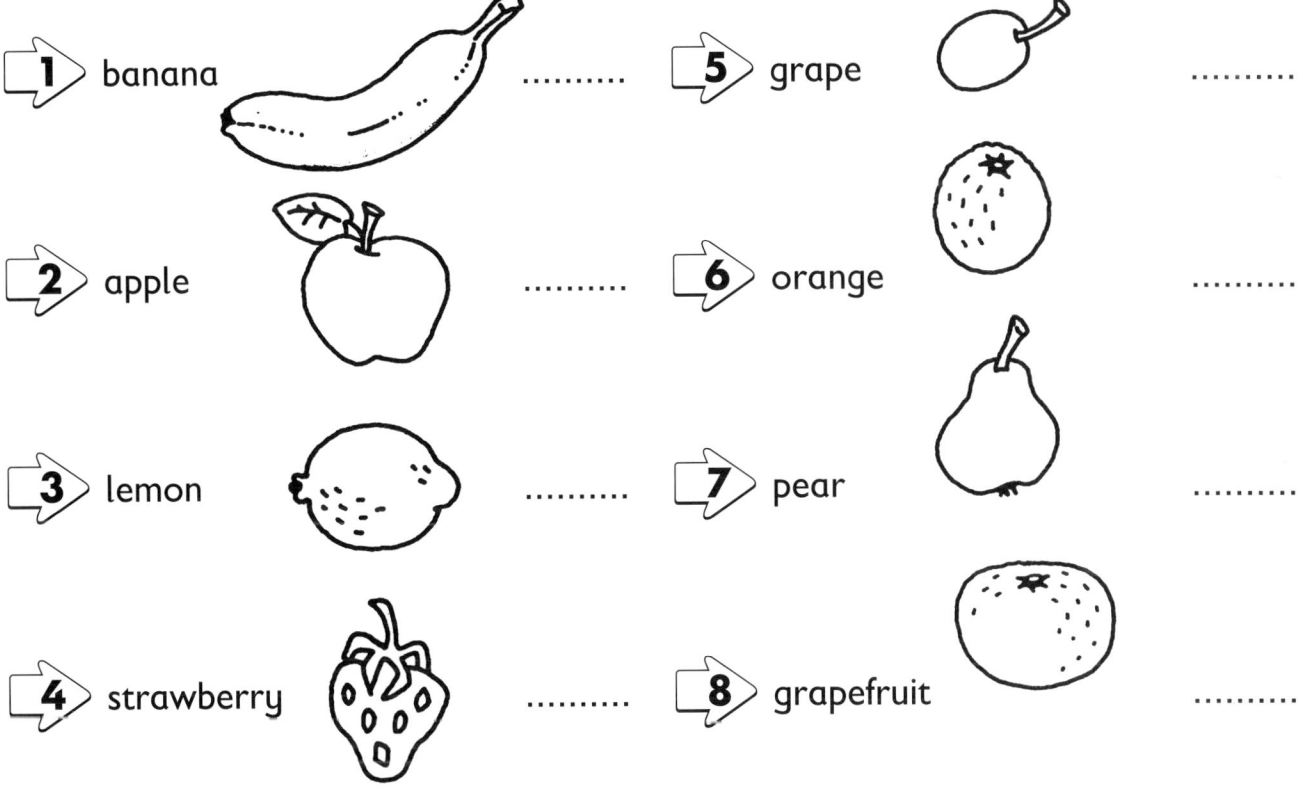

Into which boxes would these fruit be sorted?

1. banana ....
2. apple ....
3. lemon ....
4. strawberry ....
5. grape ....
6. orange ....
7. pear ....
8. grapefruit ....

? CHALLENGE Write a fruit which would be sorted into box D.

Data Handling Book 1 © Addison Wesley Longman Limited 1997

Name Class

2D Shape Tree

22
DECISION TREES

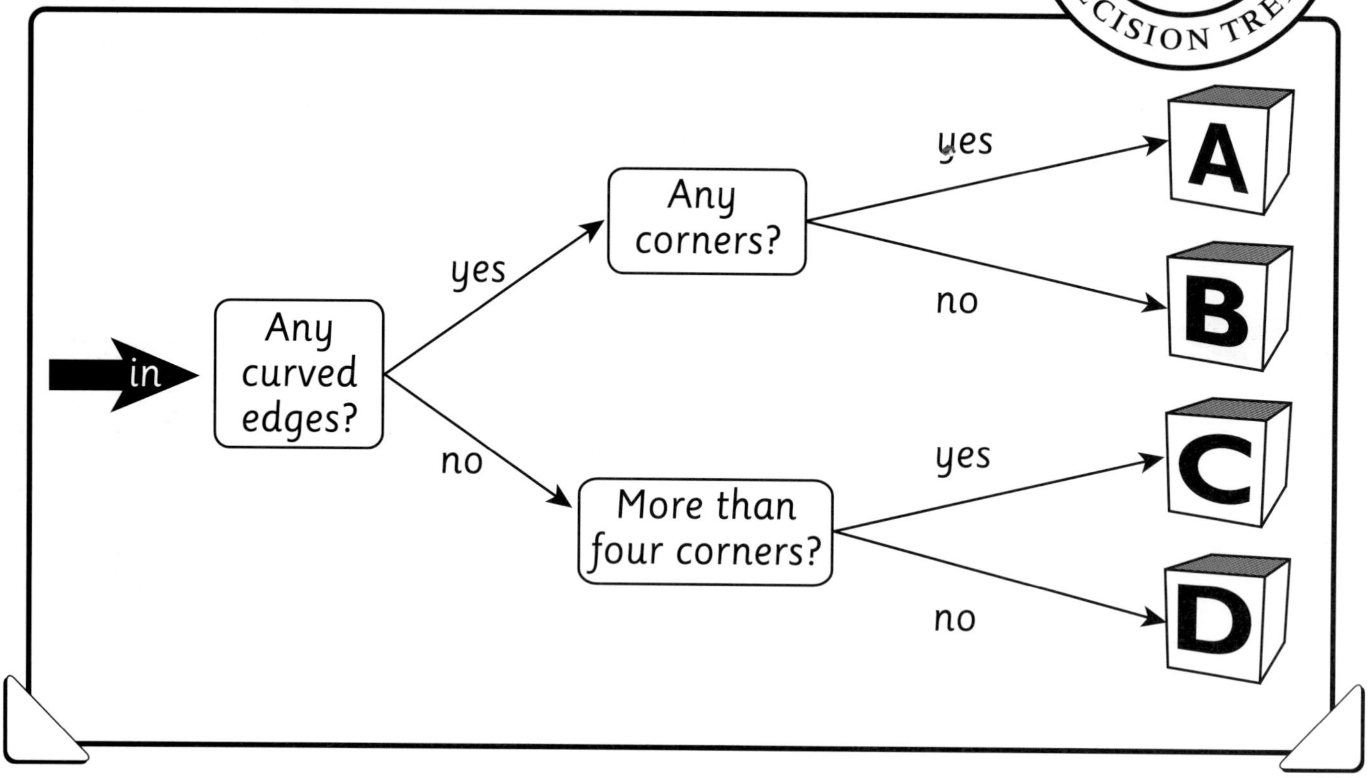

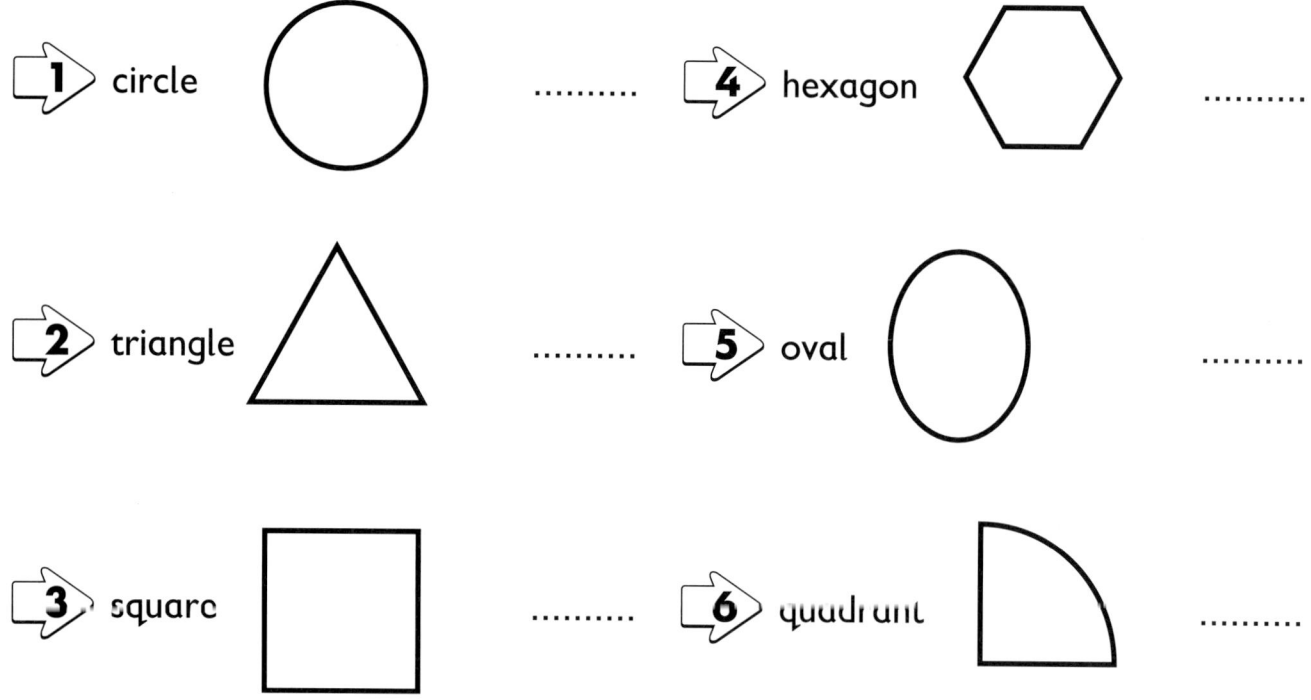

Into which box would these shapes be sorted?

1 circle ....

2 triangle ....

3 square ....

4 hexagon ....

5 oval ....

6 quadrant ....

? CHALLENGE Draw a shape which would be sorted into box C.

Name   Class

3D Shape Tree

23 DECISION TREES

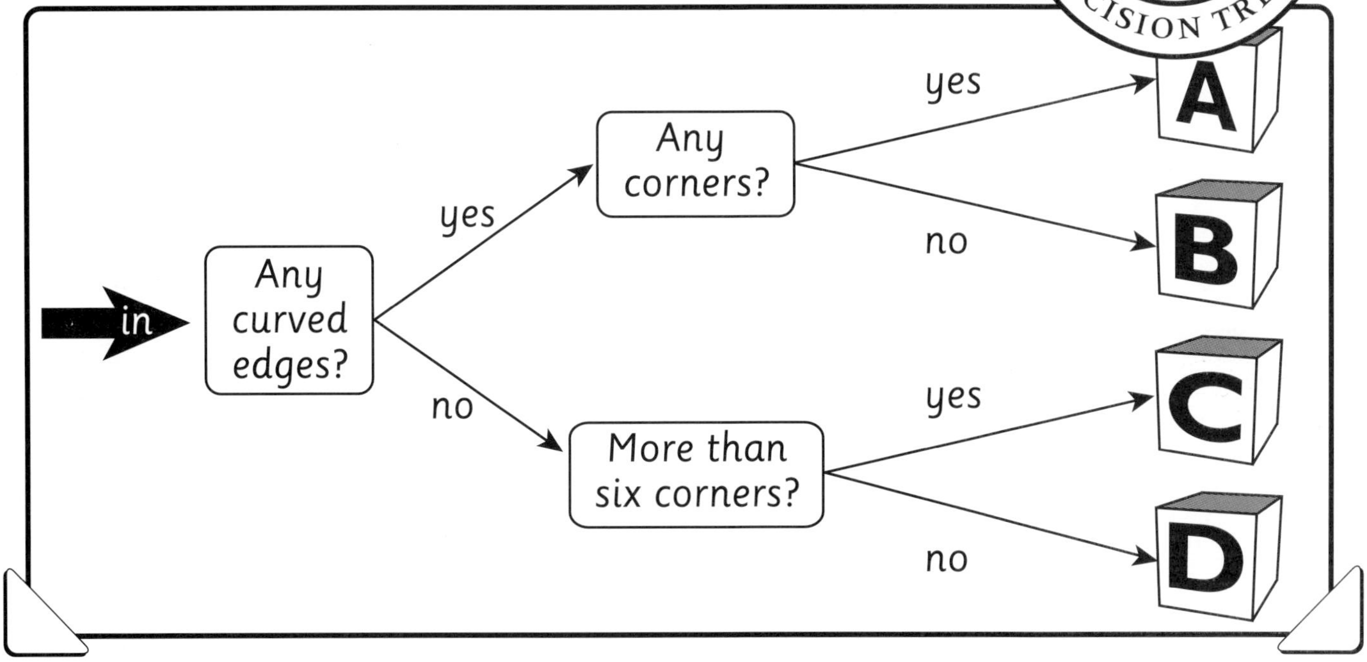

```
in → Any curved edges?
     ├─ yes → Any corners?
     │         ├─ yes → A
     │         └─ no → B
     └─ no → More than six corners?
               ├─ yes → C
               └─ no → D
```

Into which set would these shapes be sorted?

▷ **1** cube ....

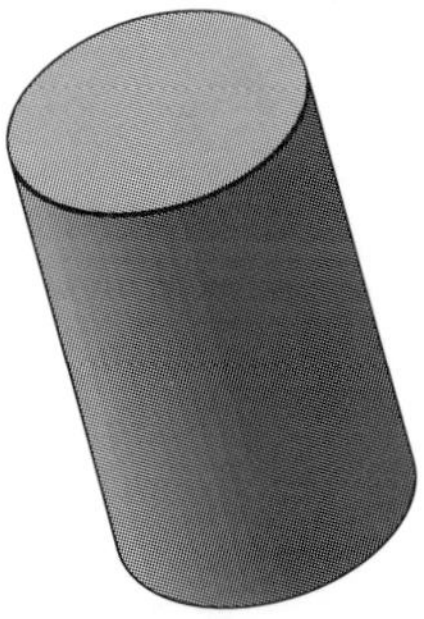

▷ **2** cone ....

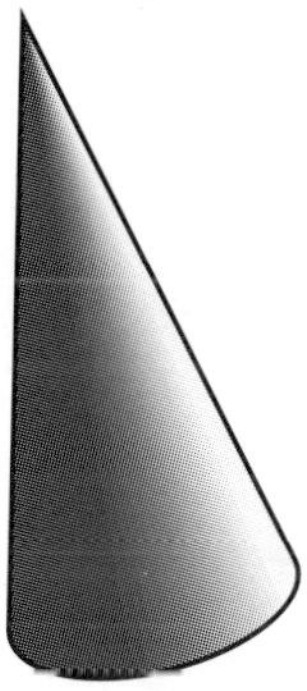

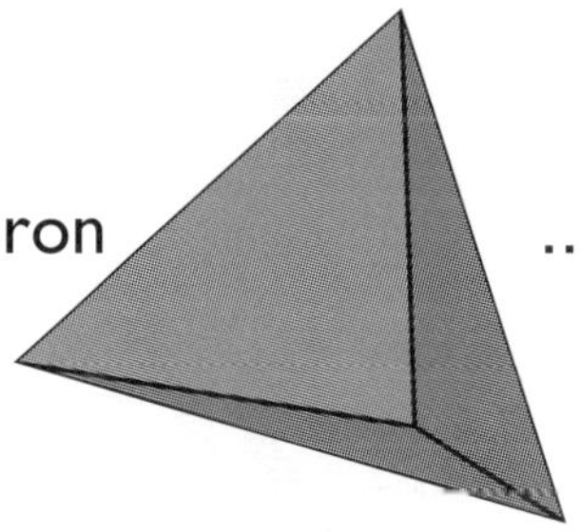

▷ **3** sphere ....

▷ **4** cylinder ....

▷ **5** tetrahedron ....

▷ **6** cuboid ....

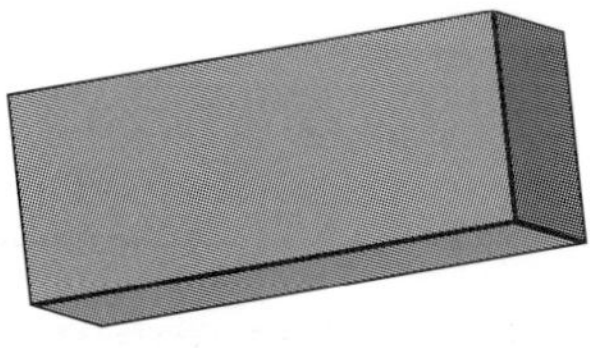

Data Handling Book 1   © Addison Wesley Longman Limited 1997

Name   Class

Number Tree

24 DECISION TREES

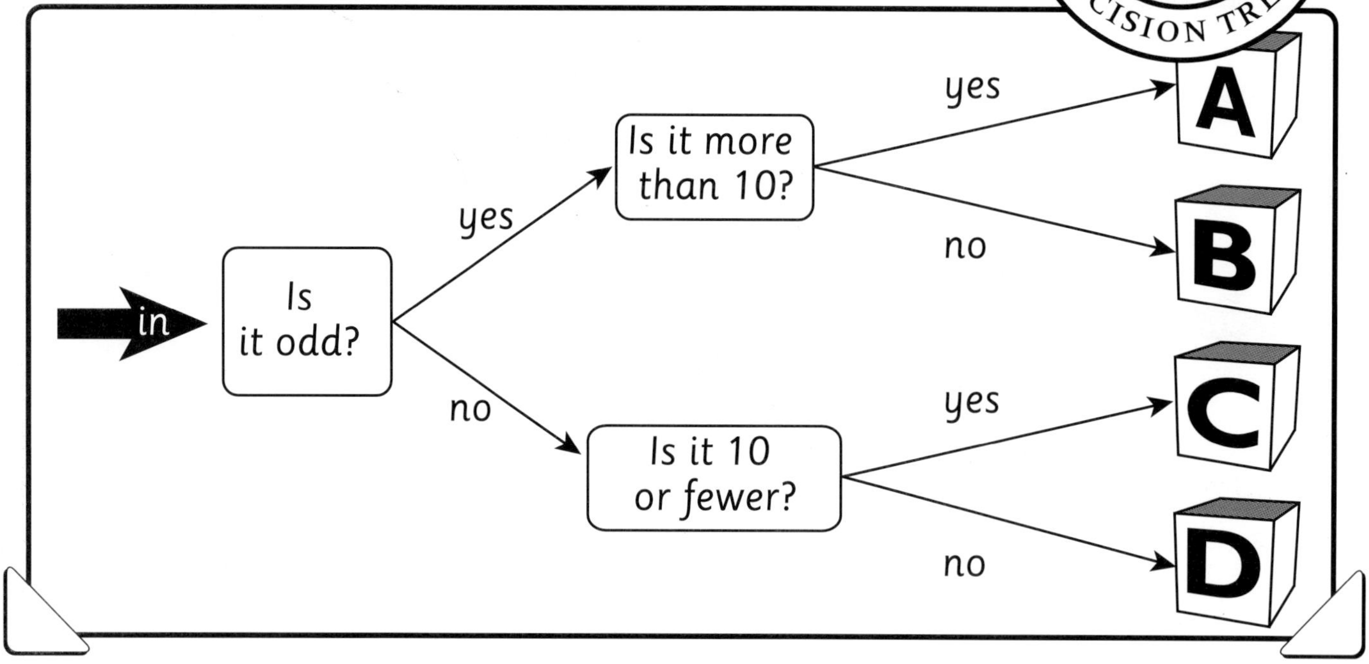

Into which sets would these numbers be sorted?

▷1 5 ....   ▷5 10 ....

▷2 4 ....   ▷6 1   ....

▷3 17 ....   ▷7 33 ....

▷4 20 ....   ▷8 50 ....

 Write a number which would be sorted into set B.

Data Handling Book 1   © Addison Wesley Longman Limited 1997

Name　　　　　　　　　　　　Class

Clown Types

25 CHARTS/LISTS & TABLES

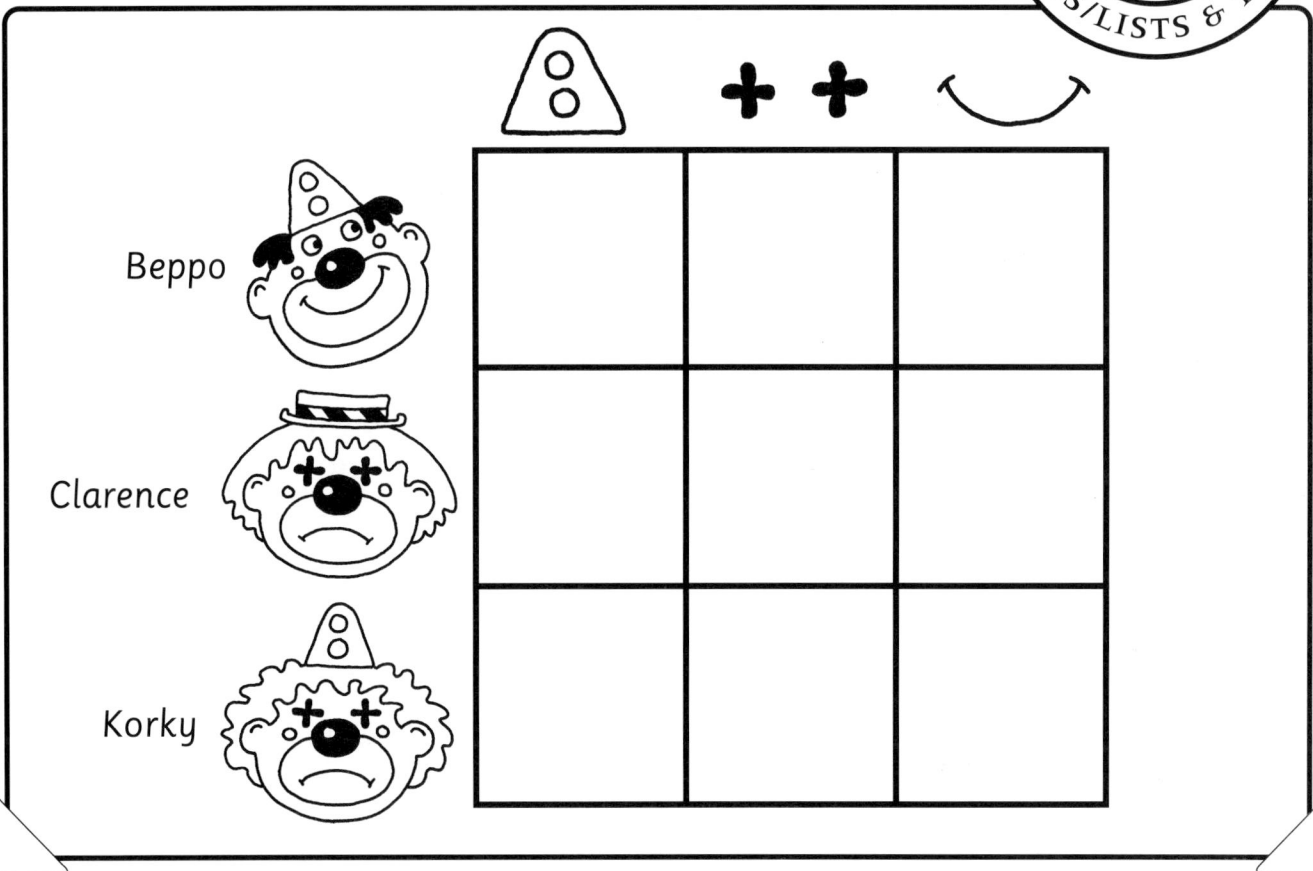

1. Tick what is special about each clown. ✓
2. Which clown looks happy?　　　　...
3. Which clown has a flat hat?　　　　...
4. Which clown has fewest ticks?　　　...

? CHALLENGE Draw a clown which would have three ticks.

Data Handling Book 1　　　　　　© Addison Wesley Longman Limited 1997

Name				Class	

Monthly Planner

26 CHARTS/LISTS & TABLES

Here is Hannah's planner for one month.

Monday		7	14 Visit Henry	21 Caravan	28 Start school
Tuesday	1 Guides	8 Mum's birthday Guides	15 Guides	22 Caravan	29 Guides
Wednesday	2	9	16	23 Caravan	30
Thursday	3 Piano	10 Piano	17 Piano	24 Caravan	
Friday	4 Swimming	11 Swimming	18 School play Break up	25 Caravan	
Saturday	5	12	19 Get ready for holiday	26 Caravan	
Sunday	6	13 Visit Grandpa	20 Caravan	27 Back from holiday	

1. Which day is Hannah's swimming lesson? ....
2. When does her school break up? ....
3. When is Hannah's mum's birthday? ....
4. What are Hannah's hobbies? ....
5. How long is she going on holiday for? ....
6. Who does she visit? ....

Data Handling Book 1 © Addison Wesley Longman Limited 1997

Our Tops

27 CHARTS/LISTS & TABLES

	John	Vijay	Teresa	Sam	Tina	Ellie	Jay
Red		✓				✓	
Yellow		✓			✓		✓
Green				✓	✓		
Blue	✓	✓	✓		✓		✓
Pink			✓				
Brown	✓						✓
Black	✓				✓		

1. Who is wearing a plain coloured top? ....
2. Who has most colours in their top? ....
3. Who has yellow in their top? ....
4. Who has no blue in their top? ....
5. Which is the most frequent colour in the tops? ....

? CHALLENGE

Colour the tops.

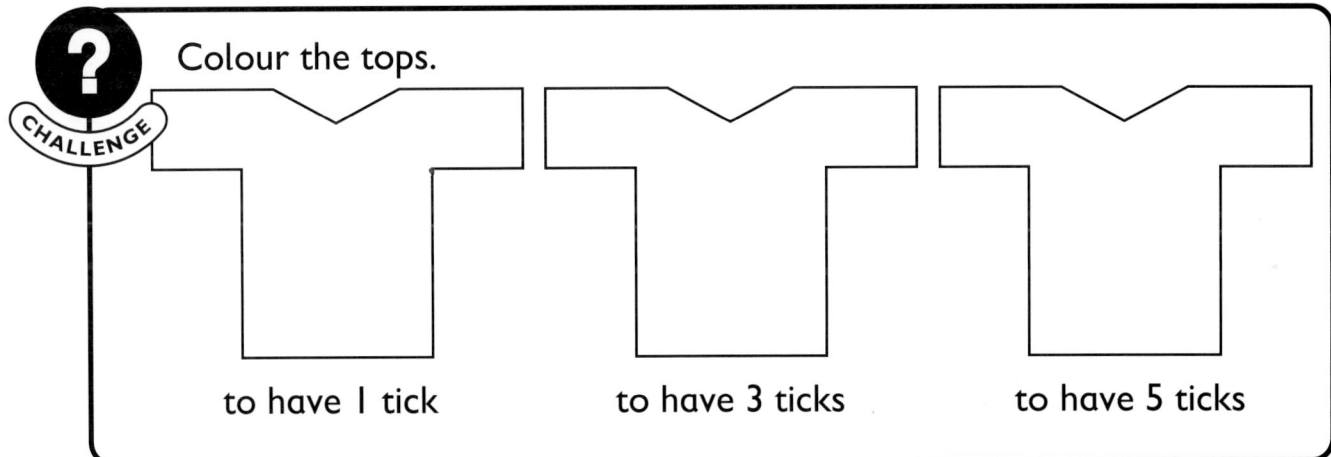

to have 1 tick   to have 3 ticks   to have 5 ticks

Data Handling Book 1   © Addison Wesley Longman Limited 1997

Name Class

Popular Children's Names 28
CHARTS/LISTS & TABLES

Boys			Girls		
	Now	Ten years ago		Now	Ten years ago
1	Thomas	Christopher	1	Rebecca	Sarah
2	James	James	2	Lauren	Laura
3	Jack	David	3	Jessica	Gemma
4	Daniel	Daniel	4	Charlotte	Emma
5	Matthew	Michael	5	Hannah	Rebecca

1) Which boy's name is most popular now? ....

2) Which boy's name was most popular ten years ago? ....

3) Which girl's name is most popular now? ....

4) Which girl's name was most popular ten years ago? ....

5) Which girl's name appears twice? ....

6) Which boys' names appear twice? ....

Data Handling Book 1 © Addison Wesley Longman Limited 1997

Name   Class

My Data

All About Me

My name   Jo Francis

My address   4 Dingle Glen, Chelmer

My phone number   0125 343 328

My birthday   25 May 1993

 What is Jo's surname? ....

 In which month is Jo's birthday? ....

 In which year was Jo born? ....

 What is Jo's telephone number? ....

 Where in Chelmer does Jo live? ....

 How old is Jo? ....

Data Handling Book 1   © Addison Wesley Longman Limited 1997

Name   Class

Record Cards

Here are some record cards.

Surname	SMITH
First name	Simon
Date of birth	24.03.77
Job	Decorator

Surname	IFFAT
First name	Nazir
Date of birth	10.12.70
Job	Doctor

Surname	FRANCIS
First name	Emma
Date of birth	14.11.73
Job	Teacher

Surname	CRAIG
First name	Susheela
Date of birth	13.09.71
Job	Baker

1. What is Emma's job? ....

2. Who is the baker? ....

3. Who was born in 1977? ....

4. What is Susheela's surname? ....

5. Who was born in December? ....

6. Who is the oldest? ....

? CHALLENGE Write your own record card.

Surname	....
First name	....
Date of birth	....
Job	....

Data Handling Book 1   © Addison Wesley Longman Limited 1997

Name   Class

Telephone Book

31

DATABASES

Here is part of a telephone directory.

Paterby P		42 Henley Rd	Flaxby	4632
Paulson F		6 Munson St	Selham	3763
Pavi S	Baker	4 High St	Munton	85432
Peabody T	Dentist	12 High St	Munton	85330
Peck D		103 West Lane	Flaxby	4607
Pedley F	Chemist	14 Elm Court	Munton	85900

1 Who is the baker? ....

2 Who lives in West Lane? ....

3 What is the address of Paul Paterby? ....

4 What is the telephone number of the dentist? ....

5 Whose telephone number is Flaxby 4607? ....

6 Where in Selham does Fiona Paulson live? ....

? CHALLENGE

Write a short telephone directory of four friends.

• ....

• ....

• ....

• ....

Name _____ Class _____

The Database

Some facts were put on a database.

32 DATABASES

Name	Sisters	Brothers	Pets	Road type	Hobbies
Ian	1	1	0	street	computer
Gregory	0	0	dog	avenue	dancing
Anil	2	1	0	avenue	football
Simon	1	0	cat	crescent	reading
Annabel	0	1	goldfish	close	swimming
Gemma	1	3	dog	road	computer
Ming Chu	0	1	dog	square	reading

1. Which children have no brothers? ....
2. Whose hobby is swimming? ....
3. Who has no pets? ....
4. Who has one sister and likes reading? ....
5. Who lives on an avenue and has a dog? ....
6. Who has a pet and plays on the computer? ....

Data Handling Book 1 © Addison Wesley Longman Limited 1997

Name   Class

Toys

The graph shows toy animals on a farm.

1. How many horses? ....
2. How many sheep? ....
3. What are there six of? ....
4. How many animals altogether? ....
5. Name two farm animals which could be birds. ....
6. In real life is a sheep as large as a horse? ....

Data Handling Book 1   © Addison Wesley Longman Limited 1997

| Name | Class |

Vegetables

Here is a graph of some children's favourite vegetables.

PICTOGRAMS 34

peas	🫛 🫛 🫛 🫛 🫛 🫛 🫛 🫛
beans	🫘 🫘 🫘 🫘
carrots	🥕 🥕 🥕 🥕 🥕 🥕
cabbage	🥬 🥬 🥬 🥬
cauliflower	🥦

1 ▷ How many children liked beans best? ....

2 ▷ How many children liked carrots best? ....

3 ▷ Which was the most popular vegetable? ....

4 ▷ Which was the least favourite vegetable? ....

5 ▷ How many children were asked about their favourite vegetable? ....

6 ▷ Write the order of popularity for the most liked vegetable to the least liked.

....
Most ━━━━━━━━━━━━━━▶ Least

Data Handling Book 1 © Addison Wesley Longman Limited 1997

Name　　　　　　　　　　　　　Class

Jelly Babies

The graph shows how many jelly babies are in a box.

Red	👶 👶 👶 👶 👶
Green	👶 👶 ⌇
Yellow	👶 👶 👶
Orange	👶 👶 👶 ⌇
Pink	👶
Purple	👶 👶 👶 👶

👶 = 2 jelly babies

1. Which is the most common colour? ....

2. Which is the least common colour? ....

3. How many green jelly babies are there? ....

4. How many orange jelly babies are there? ....

CHALLENGE How many jelly babies are there altogether?

Data Handling Book 1　　　　　　　　© Addison Wesley Longman Limited 1997

Name   Class

Pedestrians

The graph shows people seen entering shops between 11.00 am and 11.30 am.

Supermarket	👤👤👤👤👤
Chemist's	👤👤👤 (½)
Jeweller's	(½)
Shoe shop	👤 (½)
Baker's	👤👤👤👤

👤 = 10 pedestrians

(½) = less than 10 pedestrians

1 Which was the most visited shop? ....

2 Which was the least visited shop? ....

3 How many people entered the baker's? ....

4 How many people entered the chemist's? ....

5 Could the same people have entered more than one shop? ....

6 Do you think it would have been busier at 9 am? ....

Data Handling Book 1   © Addison Wesley Longman Limited 1997

Name .... Class ....

Colour Match

37

BAR GRAPH 1:1

Speech bubbles:
- I like red.
- I like red.
- Red is my choice.
- My favourite is blue.
- I like green.
- Green is my favourite.
- I like blue too.
- Yellow is my favourite.
- I like blue.
- Red is best for me.

Grid columns: Red, Yellow, Green, Blue

1 Show the favourite colours on the grid.

2 What is the most popular colour? ....

3 What is the least popular colour? ....

4 How many children like green best? ....

5 How many children like blue best? ....

6 How many children were asked about their favourite colour? ....

Data Handling Book 1 © Addison Wesley Longman Limited 1997

Name .... Class ....

The Bird Table

38
BAR GRAPH 1:1

Blue tit	☐☐☐☐☐☐☐☐
Sparrow	☐☐☐☐
Robin	☐
Starling	☐☐☐☐☐☐☐☐☐☐
Blackbird	☐☐
Doves	☐☐☐

▷ 1 How many sparrows visited? ....

▷ 2 How many starlings visited? ....

▷ 3 Which bird was most frequent? ....

▷ 4 Which bird was least frequent? ....

▷ 5 How many more starlings than doves? ....

▷ 6 How many birds altogether? ....

? **CHALLENGE** Which bird does not like other similar birds being in the same garden?

....

Data Handling Book 1 © Addison Wesley Longman Limited 1997

Name   Class

Crisps

The graph shows the favourite crisps of Class 2A.

[Bar graph showing: Plain = 8, Salt & vinegar = 6, Cheese and onion = 5, Roast chicken = 3, Prawn = 1]

1 How many children liked plain crisps best? ....

2 How many children liked roast chicken crisps best? ....

3 Which was the least popular flavour? ....

4 Which was the most popular flavour? ....

5 Did more children like prawn and roast chicken than cheese and onion? ....

6 How many children are in Class 2A? ....

Data Handling Book 1   © Addison Wesley Longman Limited 1997

Name Class

Coffee

40

BAR GRAPH 1:1

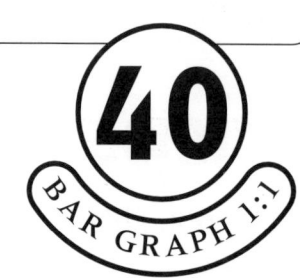

The graph shows the cups of coffee drunk by teachers in one day.

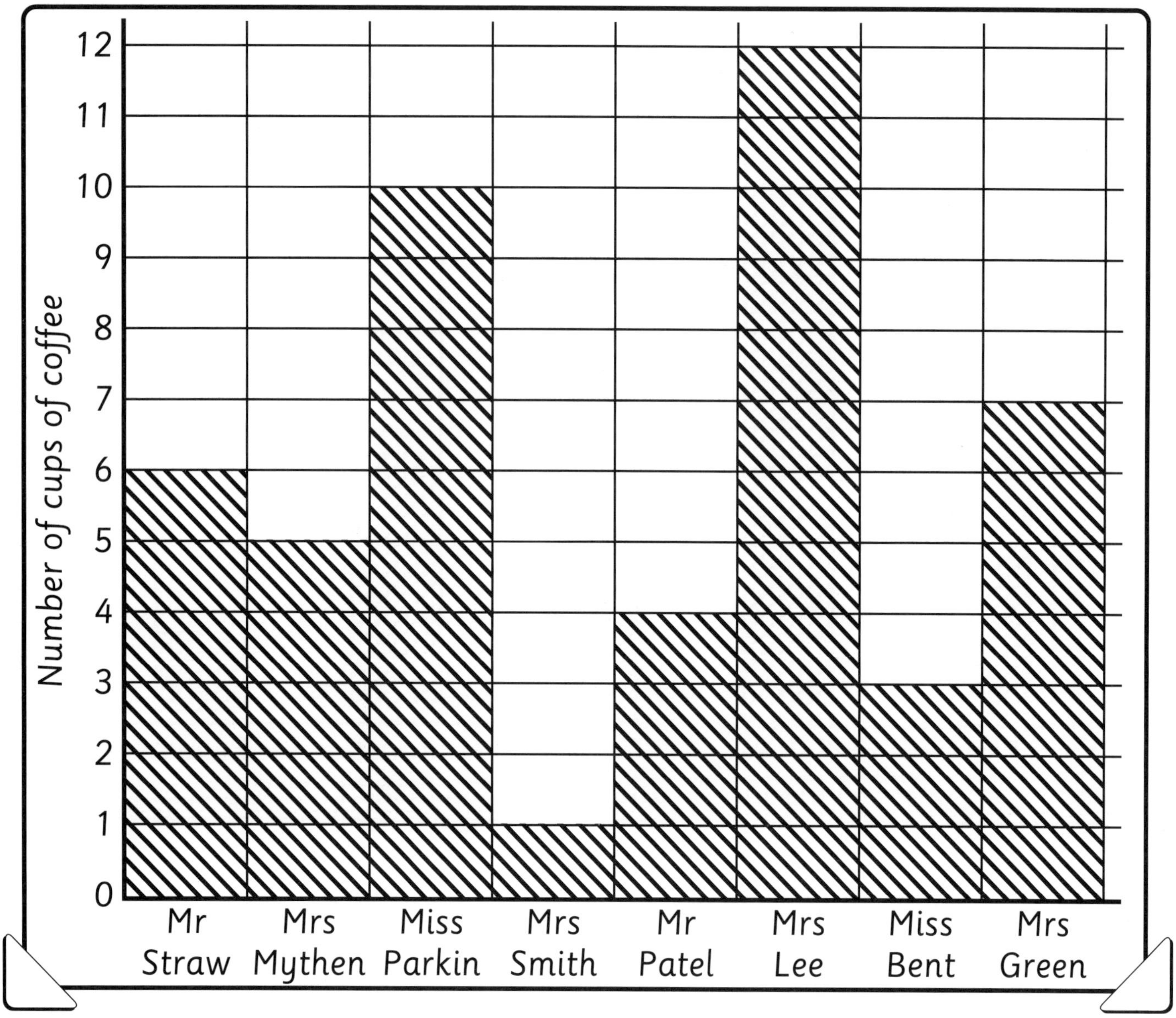

12
11
10
9
8
7
6
5
4
3
2
1
0
Number of cups of coffee
Mr Straw
Mrs Mythen
Miss Parkin
Mrs Smith
Mr Patel
Mrs Lee
Miss Bent
Mrs Green

1. Who likes coffee the most? ....
2. Who does not like coffee very much? ....
3. How many cups does Mrs Mythen drink? ....
4. Who drinks fewer than four cups of coffee? ....
5. Who drinks more than seven cups of coffee? ....

Name _____ Class _____

Favourite Activities

Some children were asked about their favourite activities.

BAR GRAPH 1:2

[Bar graph showing Number of children (0 to 12):
- Computer: 12
- Football: 9
- Swimming: 4
- Gym: 7
- Horse Riding: 5
- Singing: 8]

1 Which activity was chosen the most? ....

2 How many children chose horse riding? ....

3 Which activity did seven children choose? ....

4 Which activities were chosen by more than six children? ....

5 Which activities were chosen by fewer than five children? ....

6 What was the total for swimming and gym? ....

Data Handling Book 1 © Addison Wesley Longman Limited 1997

Name   Class

Sunshine

The graph shows hours of sunshine in one week.

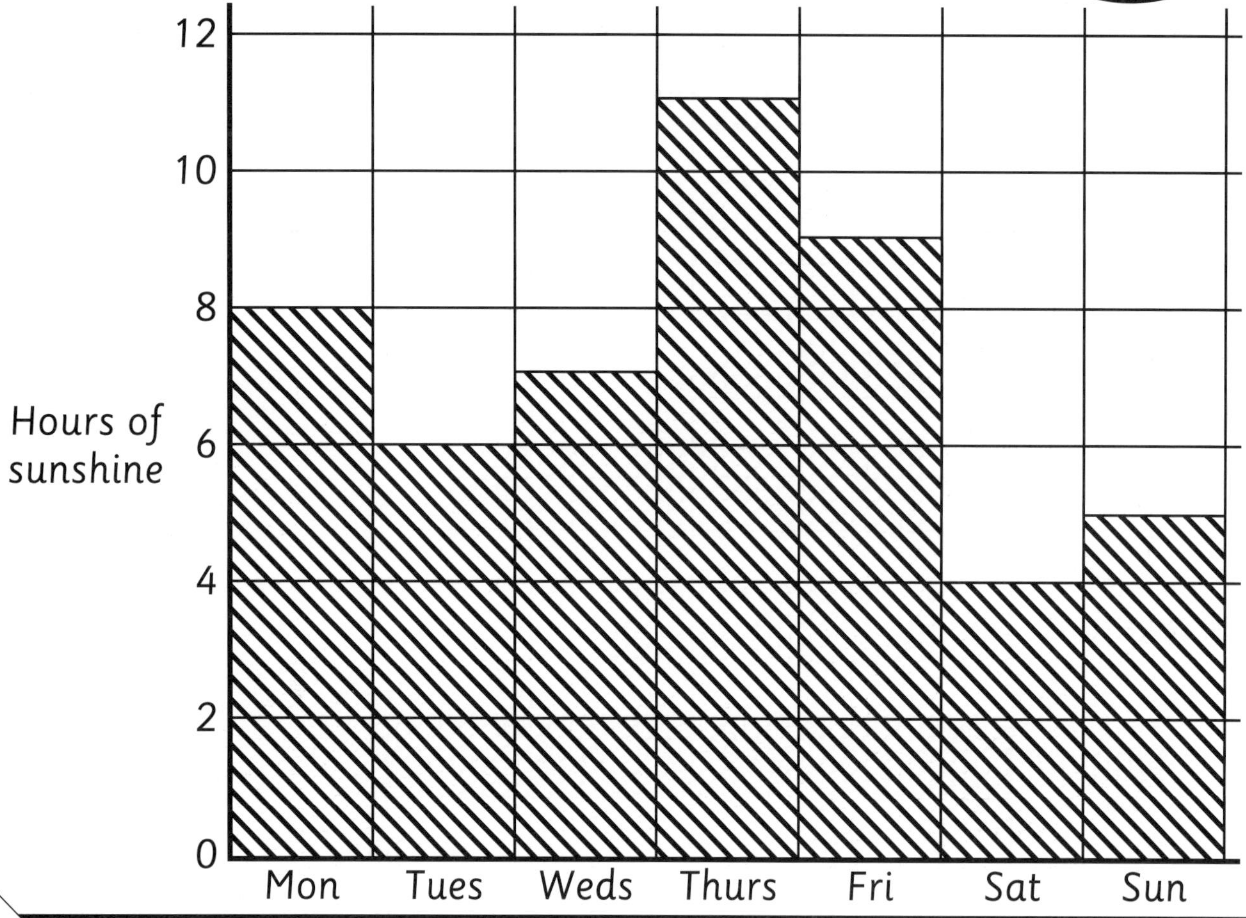

[Bar graph: Mon=8, Tues=6, Weds=7, Thurs=11, Fri=9, Sat=4, Sun=5. Y-axis: Hours of sunshine, 0 to 12.]

1. Which day was most sunny? ....

2. Which day was least sunny? ....

3. How many hours of sunshine were there on Tuesday? ....

4. How many hours of sunshine were there on Friday? ....

5. Which day had seven hours of sunshine? ....

6. Which days had more than seven hours of sunshine? ....

Data Handling Book 1   © Addison Wesley Longman Limited 1997

Name Class

Reading Books

43

BAR GRAPH 1:2

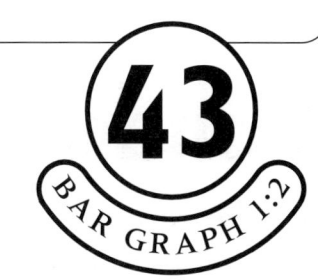

The graph shows number of books read by some children in one month.

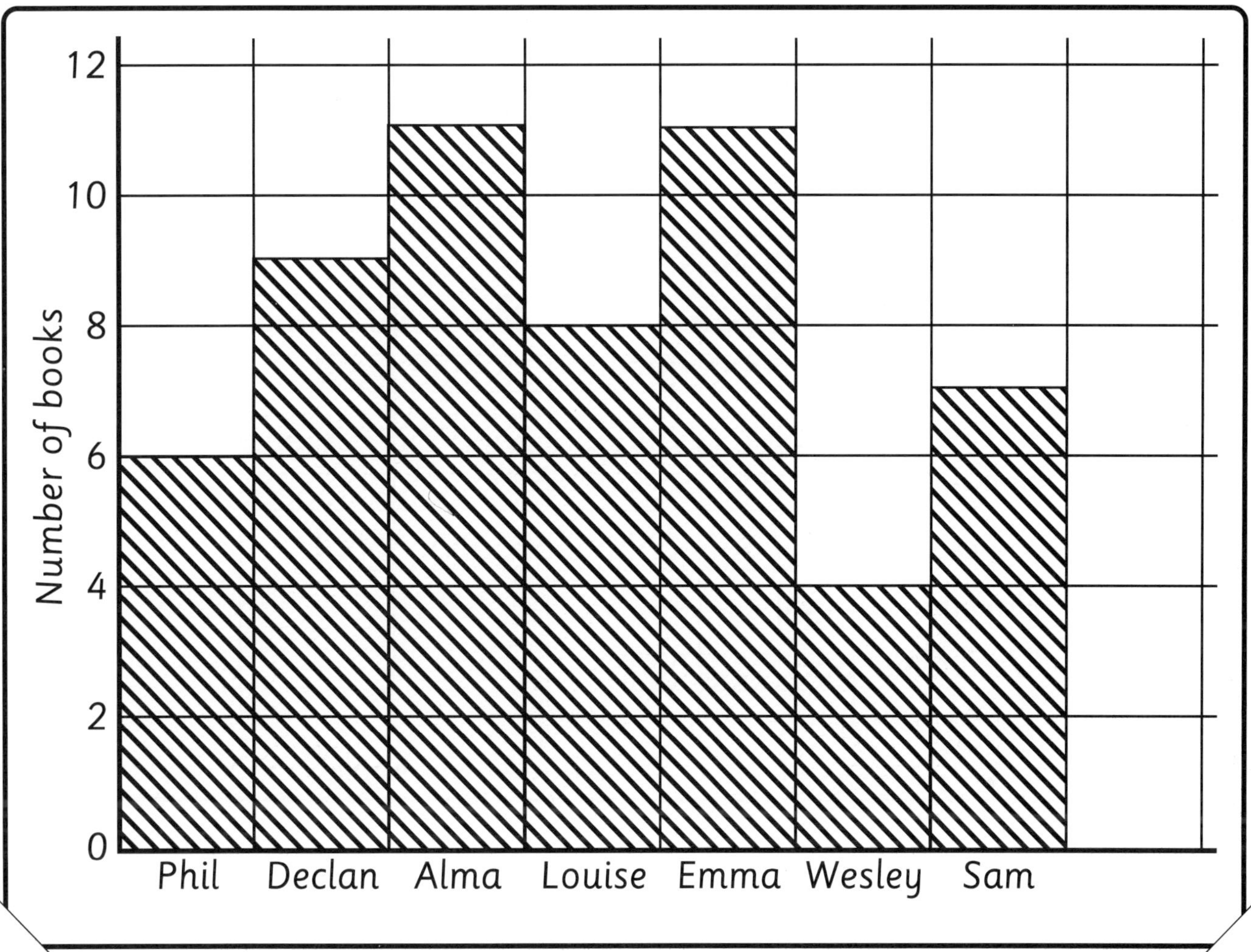

1. Who read fewest books? ....

2. How many books did Louise read? ....

3. How many books did Sam read? ....

4. Who read more than eight books? ....

5. Who read fewer than six books? ....

6. Yasin read nine books.
   Show this on the graph.

Name　　　　　　　　　　　　　Class

Holidays

People were asked about which month they go on holiday.

Holiday months

(Bar graph showing number of people going on holiday each month, x-axis 0 to 10 "Number of people")

- January: 7
- Febuary: 6
- March: 0
- April: 1
- May: 3
- June: 8
- July: 7
- August: 10
- September: 8
- October: 7
- November: 1
- December: 3

1 Which month was most popular? ....

2 Which month was least popular? ....

3 How many people went on holiday in September? ....

4 How many people went on holiday in July? ....

5 Which are the three most popular holiday months? ....

6 In which months did fewer than four people go on holiday? ....

Name   Class

Flower Bed

45

BAR GRAPH 1:10

George measured the heights of flowers in his flower bed.

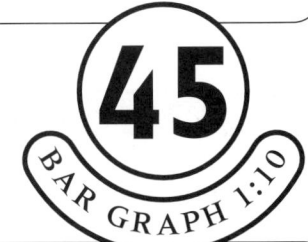

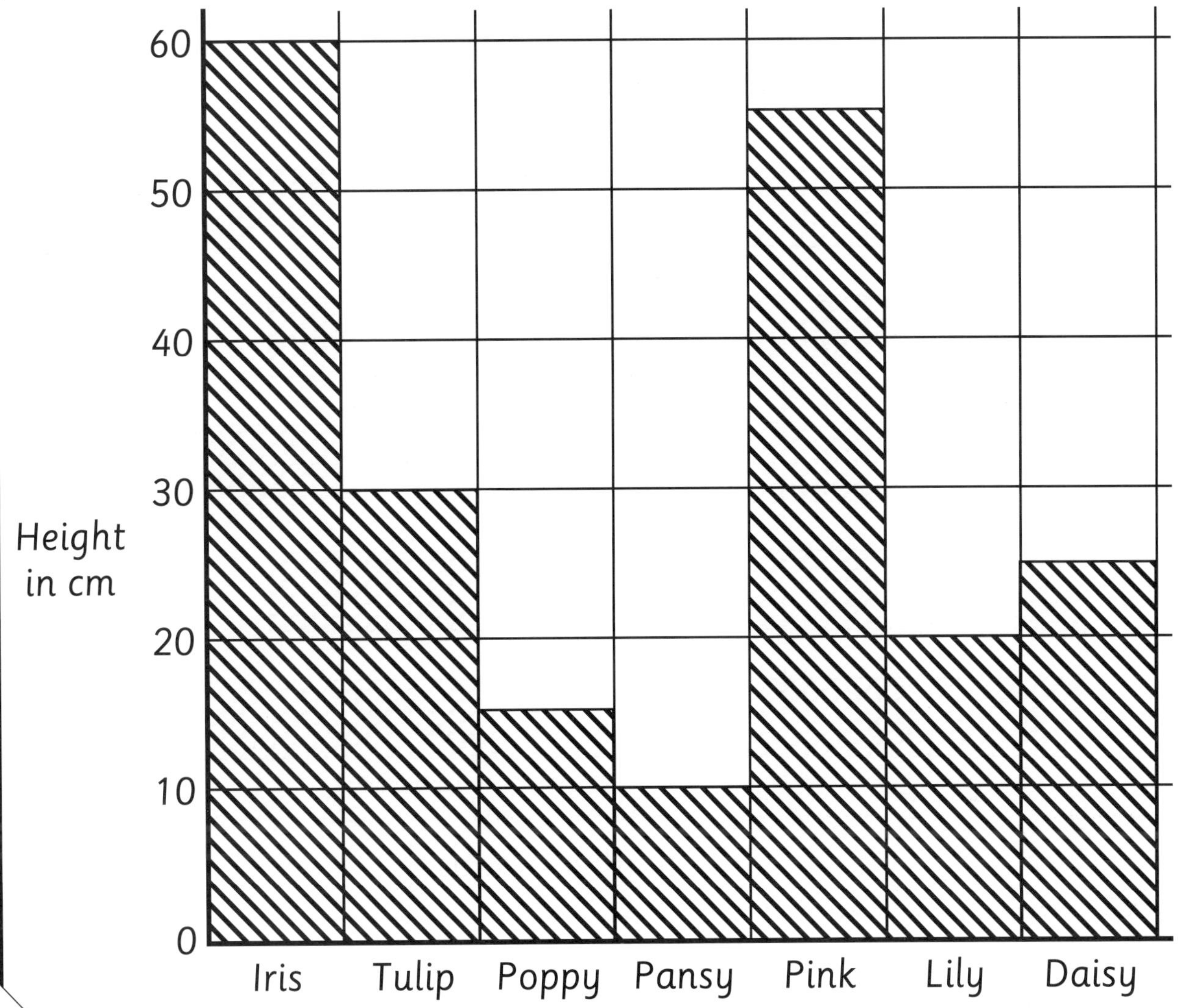

1 Which was the tallest flower? ....

2 Which was the shortest flower? ....

3 How tall was the lily? ....

4 How tall was the pink? ....

5 Which flowers were taller than 35 cm? ....

6 Which flowers were shorter than 20 cm? ....

Sponsored Laps

Some children took part in a sponsored walk round a field.

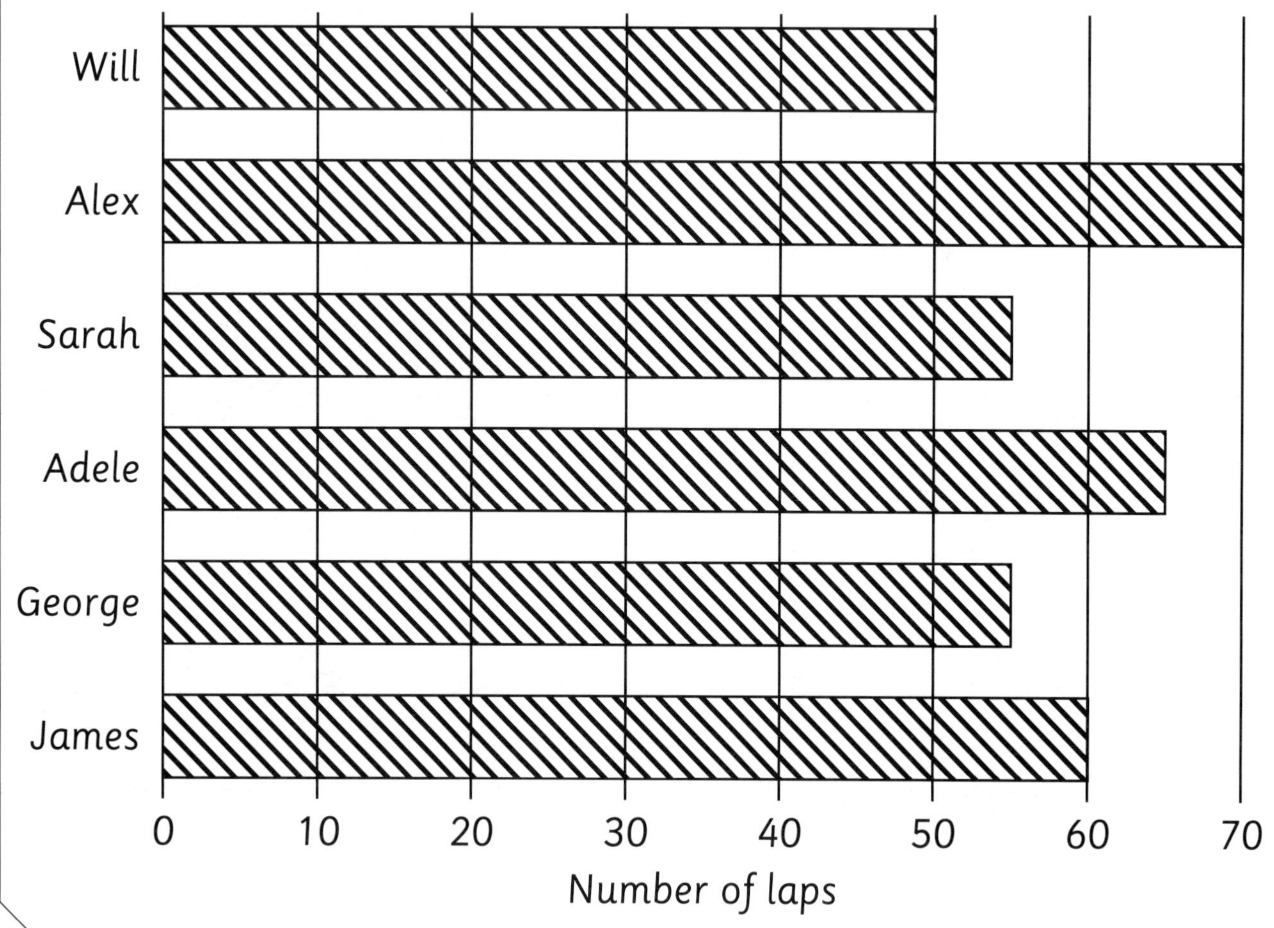

[Bar graph showing Number of laps:
- Will: 50
- Alex: 70
- Sarah: 55
- Adele: 65
- George: 55
- James: 60]

1. Who walked most laps? ....

2. Who walked fewest laps? ....

3. Who walked more than sixty laps? ....

4. Who walked fewer than fifty-five laps? ....

5. Which two children walked the same number of laps? ....

6. What was the difference in the number of laps which George walked compared to Alex? ....

Name   Class

House Visitors

The graph shows the number of visitors to a historical house in one week.

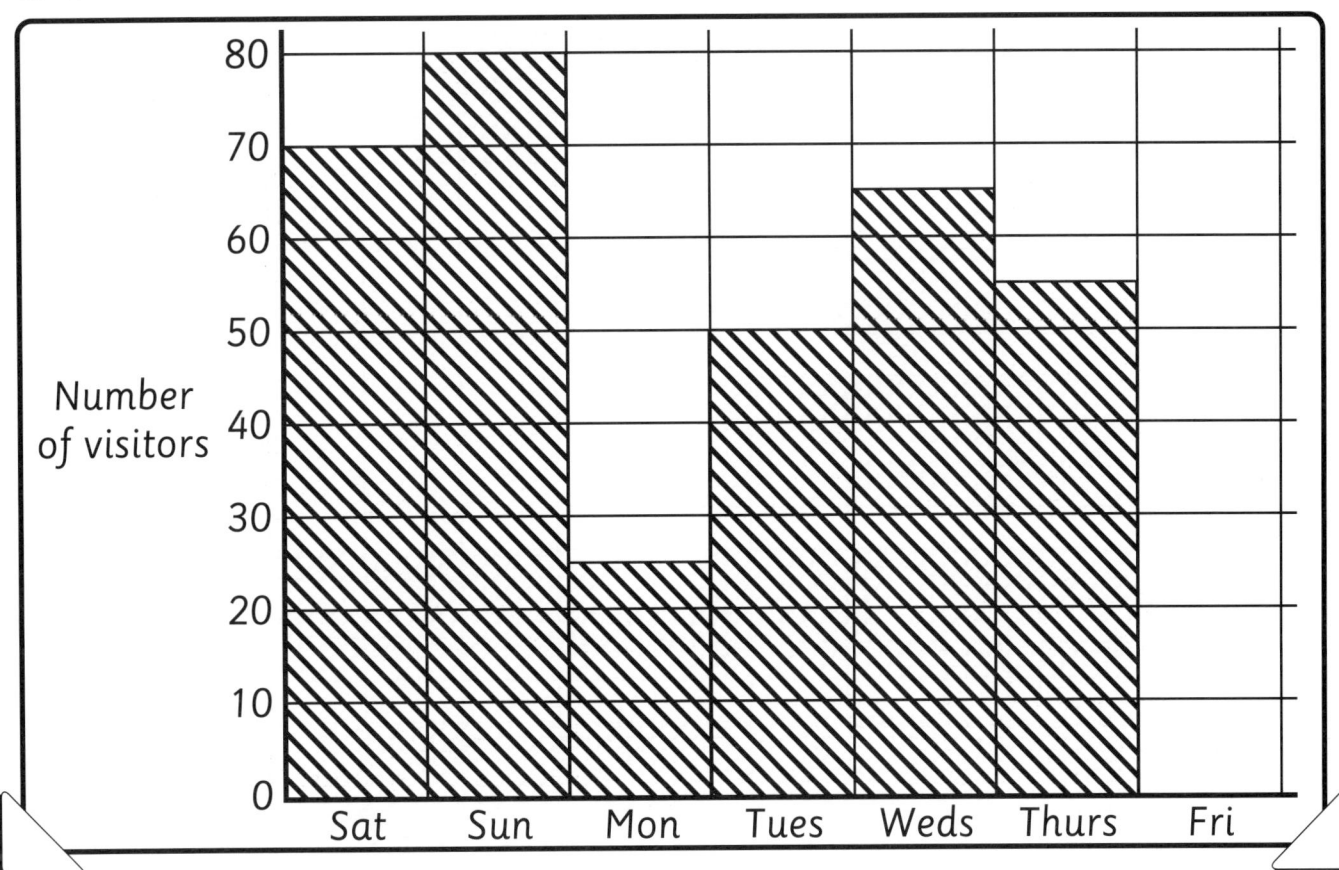

1 On which day did the
greatest number of people visit? ....

2 How many people visited on Monday? ....

3 How many people visited on Wednesday? ....

4 On which days did more
than sixty people visit? ....

5 On which days did fewer
than thirty people visit? ....

6 Why do you think
no-one visited on Friday? ....

Data Handling Book 1   © Addison Wesley Longman Limited 1997

Labels

The graph shows the labels collected by a school.

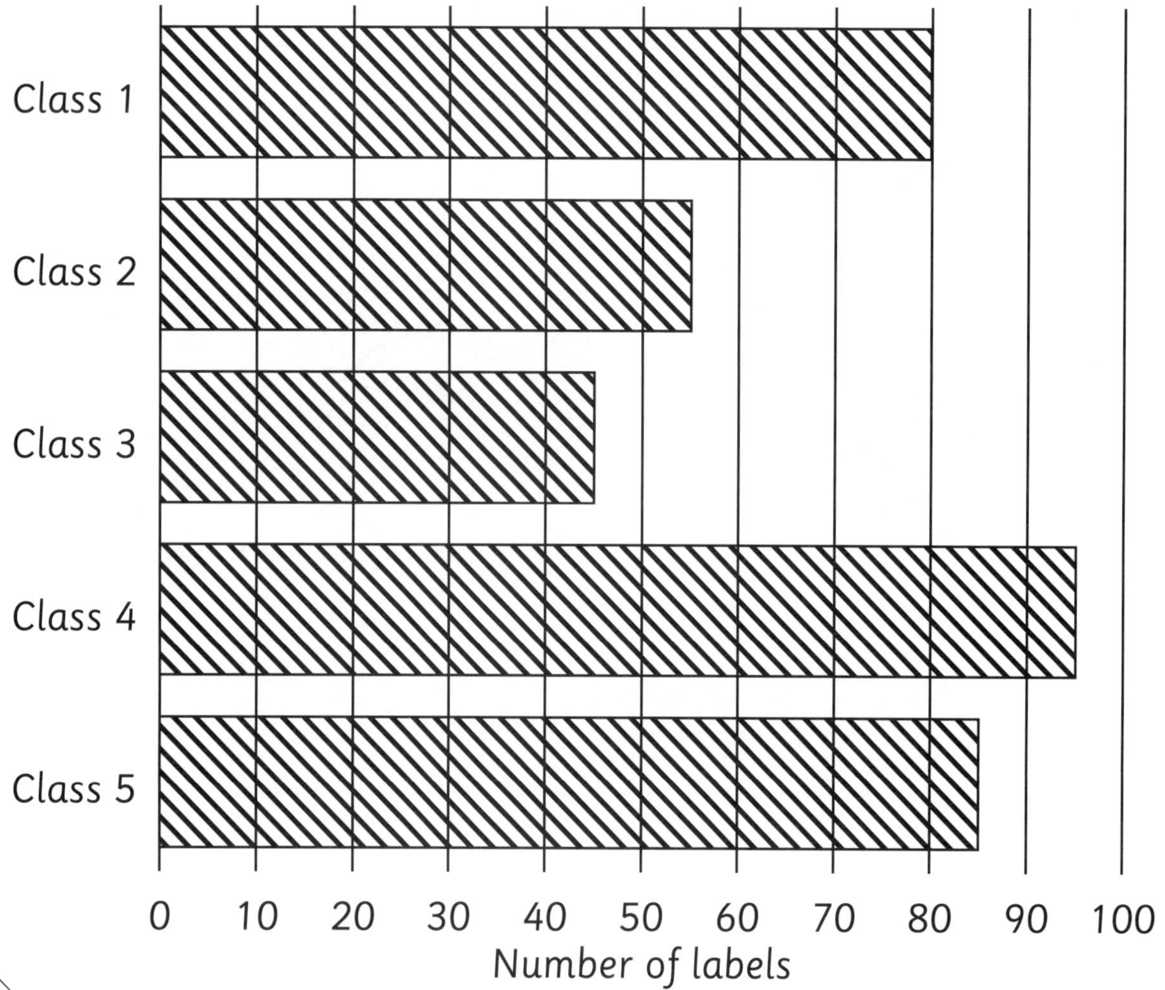

[Bar graph showing:
- Class 1: 80
- Class 2: 55
- Class 3: 45
- Class 4: 95
- Class 5: 85
Number of labels]

1. Who collected most labels? ....
2. Who collected fewest labels? ....
3. How many labels did Class 5 collect? ....
4. How many labels did Class 2 collect? ....
5. Who collected more than seventy-five labels? ....
6. How many more labels are needed for Class 5 to have 100? ....

Name   Class

Footprints

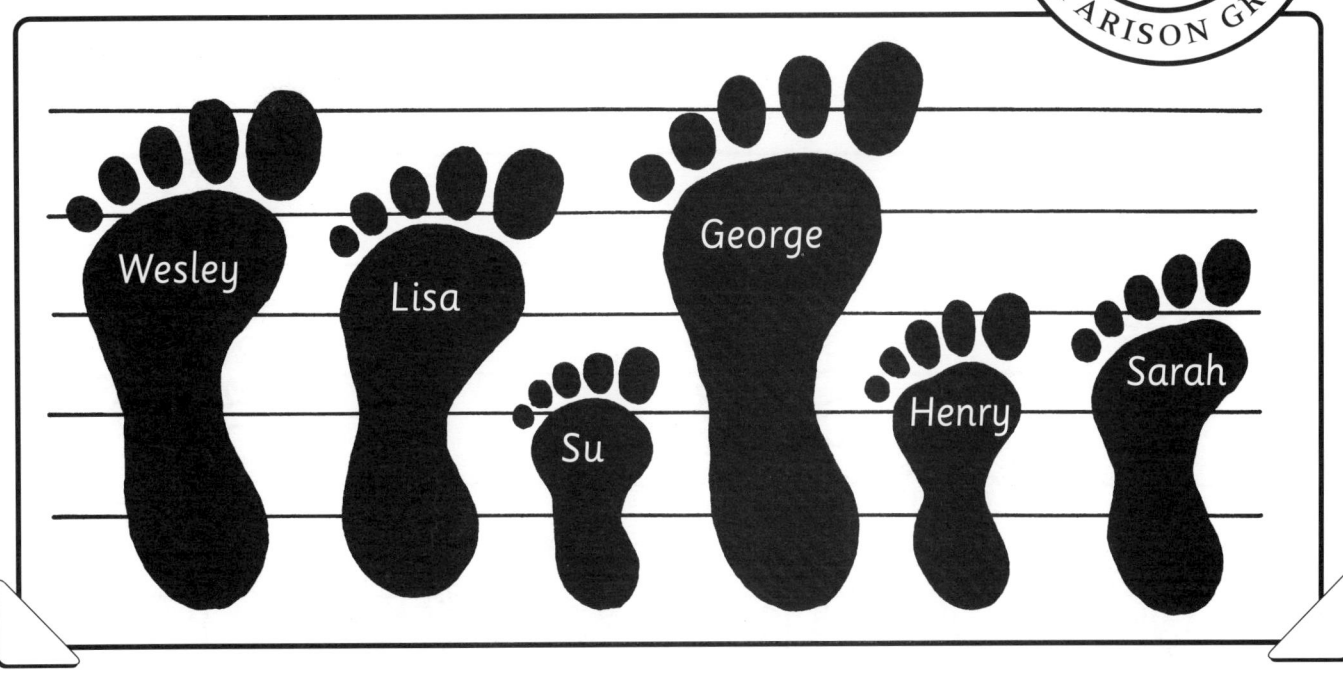

1. Who has the shortest feet? ....

2. Who has the largest feet? ....

3. Who has shorter feet than Henry? ....

4. Who has larger feet than Wesley? ....

5. Whose foot is just larger than Henry's? ....

6. List the feet in order of size from the largest to the smallest.

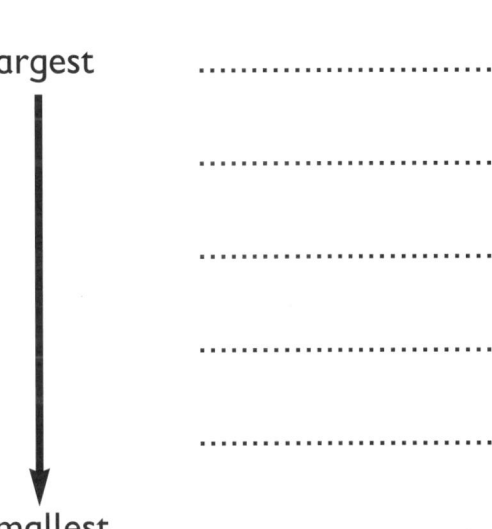

Data Handling Book 1   © Addison Wesley Longman Limited 1997

Name _____ Class _____

Flowers

50 COMPARISON GRAPHS

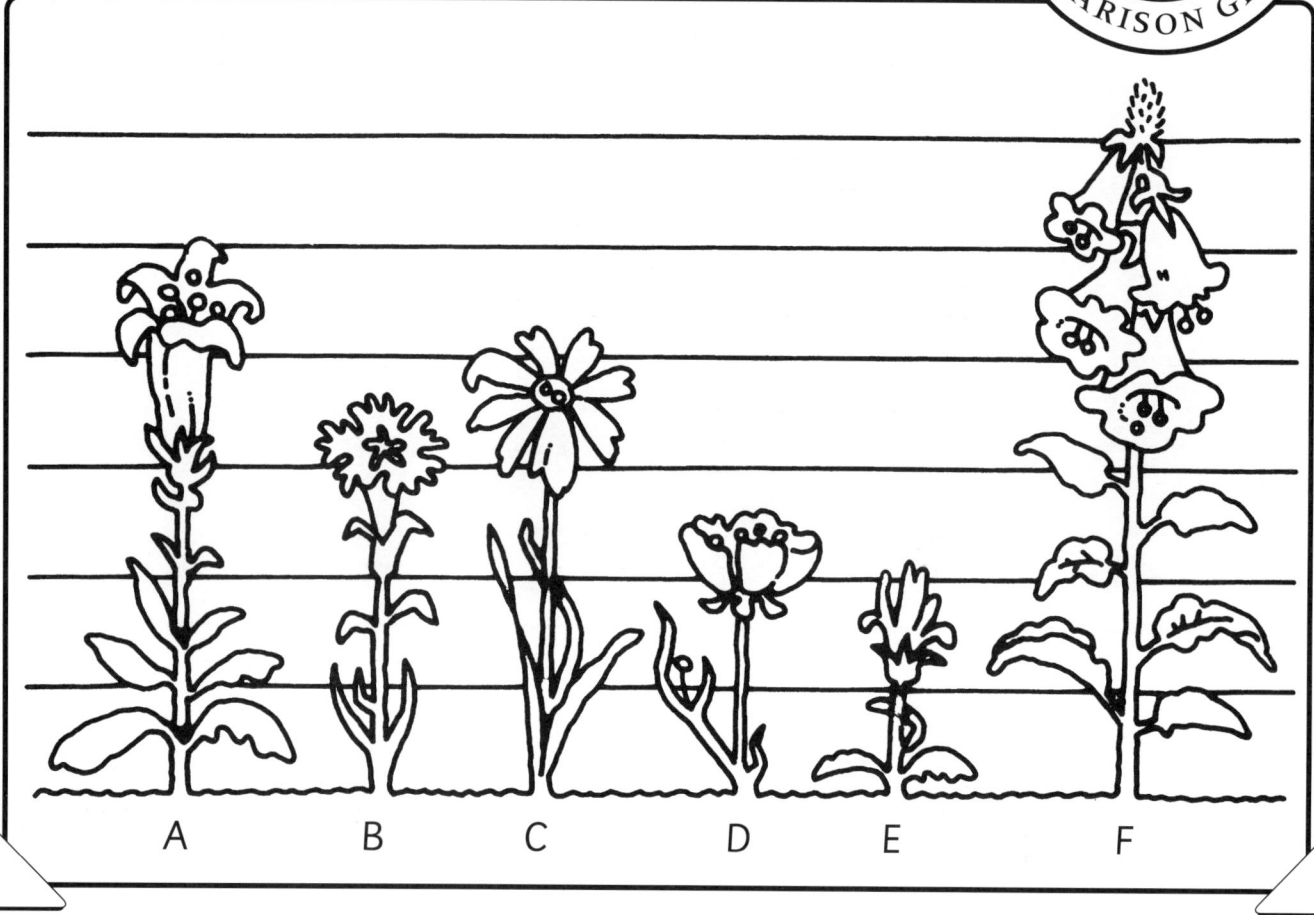

1. Which is the tallest flower? ....
2. Which is the smallest flower? ....
3. Which flowers are taller than C? ....
4. Which flowers are shorter than B? ....
5. Which flower is just shorter than A? ....
6. List the flowers in order from largest to smallest.

....

Largest ⟶ Smallest

Data Handling Book 1 © Addison Wesley Longman Limited 1997

| Name | Class |

Tins

The graph shows the circumferences of some tins.

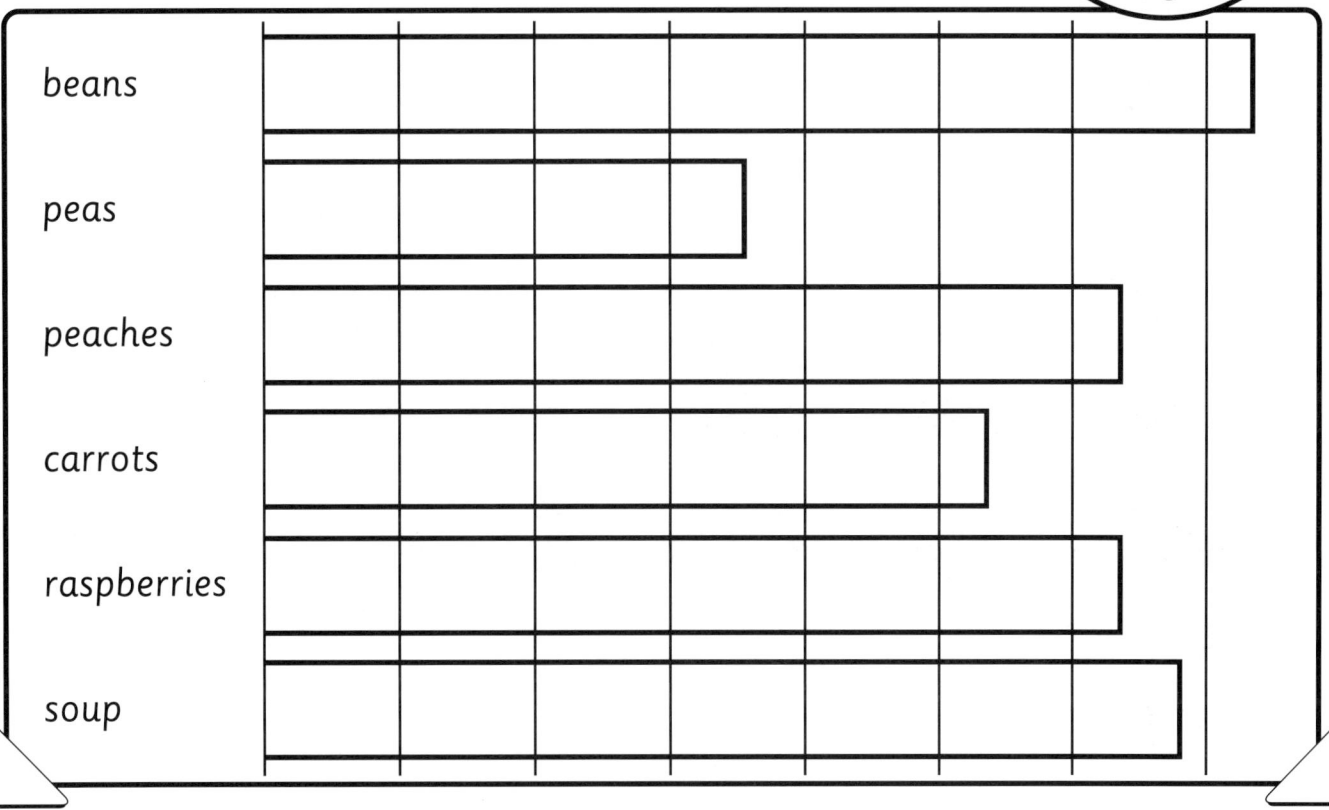

1. Which tin has the largest circumference? ....

2. Which tin has the smallest circumference? ....

3. Which tins have circumferences larger than peaches? ....

4. Which tin has a circumference smaller than carrots? ....

5. Which tin has a circumference the same as raspberries? ....

6. List the circumferences in order of size. ....

....

Smallest ⟶ Largest

Name	Class

Heights

The graph shows the shadows of some children.

1. Who is the tallest? ....

2. Who is the shortest? ....

3. Who is taller than Emily? ....

4. Who is shorter than Tamsin? ....

5. Who is about the same height as Saeed? ....

6. List the children's heights in order.

Shortest ↓ Tallest

....

....

....

....

....

....

Data Handling Book 1 © Addison Wesley Longman Limited 1997

ANSWERS

Tally Charts

 Farm Animals

1.
cows	✓✓✓✓
calves	✓✓✓
sheep	✓✓✓✓✓✓
lambs	✓✓✓✓✓
horses	✓✓✓✓✓✓✓
foals	✓✓✓✓✓

2. 7
3. 5
4. 6
5. 7
6. horses

 Lunch Boxes

1. 7
2. 9
3. 6
4. No
5. No
6. Yes

 Collecting Litter

1.
Total
18
12
8
16
9

2. 16
3. 12
4. Eg material or food bits

Challenge
 63

4 Birthday Days

1.
Total
12
20
14
10
25
13
12

2. 14
3. 20
4. Friday
5. Monday and Sunday
6. School

Display

 Fruit Bar

1. 8p
2. Banana
3. 24p
4. Lemon and strawberry
5. 18p
6. • apple and lemon
   • orange and strawberry
   • banana
   • cherries and lemon

 Clothes shop

1. £8
2. Tiger
3. Sun shade
4. £1
5. £12
6. • Sunshade glasses and spotted socks
   • FAN T-shirt
   • Striped T-shirt and plain socks
   • Sun dimmer glasses and spotted socks and plain socks
   • Tiger cap and surfer cap

 Book Shop

1. Emma Brown
2. Dinosaurs
3. Castles of Scotland
4. Things to make
5. £9
6. Adventure on DRAGO ISLAND and Lucy and the lost horse

 Multiscreen Cinemas

1. Space Family Jones
2. The Hairdresser; Space Family Jones
3. The Hairdresser; JAWS XII; Space Family Jones
4. Space Family Jones
5. Screen 1
6. 10

Venn Diagram

 Fruit Sorts
1 Two of grapes; apples or pears
2 Two of banana; orange or pineapple
3 Check child has written cherries and melon in correct place.
Challenge
Check child's answer is correct.

 Number Sort
1 Two of 21, 30 or 50
2 Two of 3, 9 or 7
3 Two of 19, 12 or 15
Challenge
Check child has written numbers in correct place.

 People Sort
1 One of Joshua, Lauren or Lee
2 One of Rebecca, Melissa or Daniel
3 One of Hannah, Ryan or Jordan
4 One of Paul, Jack or Emma
5 Jordan has blue eyes but not fair hair.
6 Jack has neither blue eyes nor fair hair.
7 Melissa has fair hair but not blue eyes.
8 Lauren has blue eyes and fair hair.
Challenge
Check that Simon's name is in the correct place.

12 **Shape Sorts**
1 Two of diamond, rectangle or arrow head
2 Two of pentagon, triangle or circle
3 Check that shapes are drawn in the correct place.
Challenge
Check child's two drawings are in the correct place.

Carroll Diagram

 Vegetable Sort
1 Underground
2 Above ground
3 Potatoes; carrots; turnips; swedes
4 Either cabbage; peas; cauliflower or beans
Challenge
Check child's two vegetables are in the correct place.

 Shape Boxes
1–6 Check child's drawings are in the correct place.
Challenge
Check child's shape is correct.

 Shoe Sort
1 One of Matthew, Ravi, or Vicky
2 One of Elena, Ian or Amy
3 One of William or Sophie
4 Elena is wearing brown shoes which do not lace up.
5 Lisa is wearing shoes which are not brown and do not lace up.
6 Matthew is wearing shoes which are not brown but lace up.
Challenge
Check child puts George in the correct place on the diagram.

 Card Sorting
1 5
2 6
3 5
4 3
5 3
6 11
Challenge
Check child draws the cards in the correct place on the diagram.

Mapping

 Sports
1 Tennis
2 Football and tennis
3 Miss Clark and Mrs Watson
4 Mr Williams
5 Tennis
6 Hockey and tennis

 Where We Live
1 Joseph
2 Rebecca
3 Avenue
4 Avenue
5 2
6 6

Challenge
   Check child has drawn name and arrow in the correct place.

 Instruments
1 Piano
2 Piano and recorder
3 Henry, Jody, Ellen
4 Jody, John, Sarah and Ellen
5 3
6 Recorder

Challenge
   Check child has recorded information in the correct place.

 Our Lunch
1 Sam
2 Kay and Sam
3 Francis
4 Bag
5 Brown
6 1
7 Kay
8 Caron and Francis

Decision Tree

 Fruit Tree
1 D
2 B
3 C
4 B
5 B
6 C
7 B
8 C

Challenge
   Check child's answer is correct.

 2D Shape Tree
1 B
2 D
3 D
4 C
5 B
6 A

Challenge
   Check child's shape is correct.

 3D Shape Tree
1 C
2 A
3 B
4 B
5 D
6 C

 Number Tree
1 B
2 C
3 A
4 D
5 C
6 B
7 A
8 D

Challenge
   Check child's answer is corrrect.

Charts/Lists and Tables

25 Clown Types
1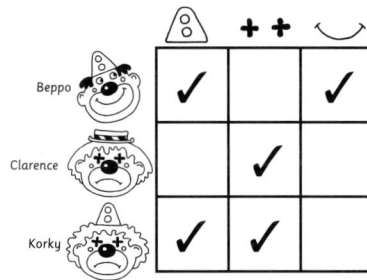
2 Beppo
3 Clarence
4 Clarence
Challenge
 Check child's drawing would have 3 ticks.

26 Monthly Planner
1 Friday
2 Friday 18th
3 Tuesday 8th
4 Piano, Guides, swimming
5 1 week
6 Grandpa and Henry

27 Our Tops
1 Sam and Ellie
2 Tina
3 Vijay, Tina and Jay
4 Sam and Ellie
5 Blue
Challenge
 Check child's answers are correct.

28 Popular Children's Names
1 Thomas
2 Christopher
3 Rebecca
4 Sarah
5 Rebecca
6 James and Daniel

Databases

29 My Data
1 Francis
2 May
3 1993
4 0125 343328
5 4 Dingle Glen
6 4

30 Record Cards
1 Teacher
2 Susheela Craig
3 Simon Smith
4 Craig
5 Nazir Iffat
6 Nazir Iffat
Challenge
 Check child's own record card.

31 Telephone Book
1 S Pavi
2 D Peck
3 42 Henley Road, Flaxby
4 Munton 85330
5 D Peck
6 6 Munson Street
Challenge
 Check child's own directory.

32 The Database
1 Gregory and Simon
2 Annabel
3 Ian and Anil
4 Simon
5 Gregory
6 Gemma

Pictograms

 Toys
1 3
2 4
3 Cows
4 18
5 Chickens and geese
6 No

 Vegetables
1 4
2 6
3 Peas
4 Cauliflower
5 23
6 Peas, carrots, beans/cabbage, cauliflower

35 **Jelly Babies**
1 Red
2 Pink
3 5
4 7
Challenge
  38

36 **Pedestrians**
1 Supermarket
2 Jeweller's
3 40
4 Between 20 and 30
5 Yes
6 No

Bar Graph 1:1

 Colour Match
1
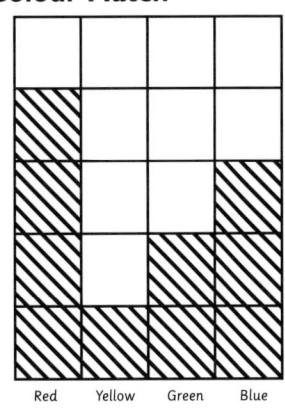
2 Red
3 Yellow
4 2
5 3
6 10

38 **The Bird Table**
1 5
2 10
3 Starling
4 Robin
5 6
6 30
Challenge
  Robin

 Crisps
1 8
2 3
3 Prawn
4 Plain
5 No
6 23

 Coffee
1 Mrs Lee
2 Mrs Smith
3 5
4 Mrs Smith and Miss Bent
5 Miss Parkin and Mrs Lee

Bar Graph 1:2

 Favourite Activities
1 Computer
2 5
3 Gym
4 Computer, football, gym and singing
5 Swimming
6 11

 Sunshine
1 Thursday
2 Saturday
3 6
4 9
5 Wednesday
6 Monday, Thursday and Friday

 Reading Books
1 Wesley
2 8
3 7
4 Declan, Alma and Emma
5 Wesley
6 Check child's answer is correct.

 Holidays
1 August
2 March
3 8
4 7
5 June, August and September
6 March, April, May, November and December

Bar Graph 1:10

 Flower Bed
1 Iris
2 Pansy
3 20 cm
4 55 cm
5 Iris and pink
6 Poppy and pansy

 Sponsored Lap
1 Alex
2 Will
3 Alex and Adele
4 Will
5 Sarah and George
6 15

 House Visitors
1 Sunday
2 25
3 65
4 Saturday, Sunday and Wednesday
5 Monday and Friday
6 It was closed.

 Labels
1 Class 4
2 Class 3
3 85
4 55
5 Class 1, Class 4 and Class 5
6 15

Comparison Graphs

 Footprints
 1 Su
 2 George
 3 Su
 4 George
 5 Sarah's
 6 George, Wesley, Lisa, Sarah, Henry, Su

 Flowers
 1 F
 2 E
 3 A and F
 4 D and E
 5 C
 6 F, A, C, B, D, E

 Tins
 1 Beans
 2 Peas
 3 Beans and soup
 4 Peas
 5 Peaches
 6 Peas, carrots, peaches/raspberries, soup, beans

 Heights
 1 Saeed
 2 Ian
 3 Saeed, Jenny, Glen, Tamsin
 4 Emily and Ian
 5 Glen
 6 Ian, Emily, Tamsin, Jenny, Glen, Saeed

Data Handling

RECORD 1

Completed Activity Sheets **Notes**

Tally Charts	1	2	3	4
Displays	5	6	7	8
Venn Diagrams	9	10	11	12
Carroll Diagrams	13	14	15	16
Mappings	17	18	19	20
Decision Trees	21	22	23	24
Charts/Lists and Tables	25	26	27	28
Databases	29	30	31	32
Pictograms	33	34	35	36
Bar Graph 1:1	37	38	39	40
Bar Graph 1:2	41	42	43	44
Bar Graph 1:10	45	46	47	48
Comparison Graphs	49	50	51	52